1967

THE CHRISTIAN
IMAGE
OF WOMAN

THE CHRISTIAN IMAGE OF WOMAN

by

Willi Moll

1314

Translated by
Elisabeth Reinecke and
Paul C. Bailey, C.S.C.

Fides Publishers, Inc.
Notre Dame, Indiana

Nihil Obstat:
Louis J. Putz, C.S.C.
University of Notre Dame

Imprimatur:
Leo A. Pursley, D.D.
Bishop of Fort Wayne-South Bend

Library of Congress Catalog
Card Number: 66-30592

Published originally in German by Verlag Styria, Graz,
under the title *Die Dreifache Antwort der Liebe*, 1964,
with the *imprimatur* of the Ordinary of Graz-Seckau.

This book is a sequel and response to *Father and Fatherhood* which introduced Willi Moll to English readers. The translators found *Father and Fatherhood* to be a very masculine and fatherly book — strong and decisive — with hands that took hold of things to bend them into shape and an intellect that expressed itself in abstract definitions and with practical insights into the work-a-day world. It was mainly a conversation between Father and Son, a man-to-man kind of book waiting for its fulfillment in the coming of the Spirit of love and the incarnation of woman.

The Christian Image of Woman is about the Holy Spirit and woman, neither of whom is primarily interested in the intellectual surgery of abstract theological, philosophical and scientific definitions but rather in letting love play its healing role in response to whoever is in need and to whatever is in need, no matter how it is worded. Hence, the translators have avoided such abstract terms as *psycho-physical union*, etc., and kept the more concrete expressions: *soul-body, the becoming-one, two-in-oneness* (even though they seem so embarrassingly clumsy), in order to make this book live, in its verbal expression, the actualities of life: spiritual, high-minded agape must be fused with sensual eros and "sordid" sex if love is to be both human *and* divine. The Holy Spirit and woman are interested in uniting and making a unity out of two substantives which are hyphenated in this life: soul-body, parent-child, husband-wife, spirit-matter . . . for they are the great *And* of all the polarities of life.

While not so masculine as *Father and Fatherhood*, this book is perhaps more truly manly since it sees the need for the man to respond, like woman, to God — if he is to have the courage to be man.

PAUL C. BAILEY, C.S.C.

CONTENTS

Chapter 1

FOUNDATION FOR A THEOLOGICAL ANTHROPOLOGY OF WOMAN

Introduction

Meditation On the Center

There are times when theology can afford to dedicate itself to matters of second and third importance, when non-essential questions can be treated seriously and honestly. In such instances, concern about certain forms of piety, or the Church's positive juridical norms for the veneration of relics or for curial politics, is reasonable enough. But other times inevitably demand reflection on the essentials. Such times urge that the central truths in danger of becoming obscured or of receding from man's consciousness be brought out of darkness and silence into light and discussion. Such a time is ours.

The consciousness of modern mankind is constantly expanding more quickly and more extensively in peripheral areas. Soon, school children will include remote stars in their process of thinking. In the face of this tremendously expanding horizon, the question of the essence, of the center, is more pressing than ever before. Not eveything is in flight yet! The centripetal powers are still stronger.

The center to be newly considered, questioned and investigated, is, and ever will be: God and man — these two — nothing else.

The Dagners of Modern Unbelief

Modern unbelief hardly ever rebels any more in Promethean defiance. It asks dispassionately: why do we need God? Haven't we got on marvelously without him? Are we not also happy without this center? In former centuries, disbelief appeared in the garb of apostasy; today it manifests itself in a gradual slipping into vagueness. Atheism has entered an existential phase in which intellectual argument has become almost superfluous. More and more areas of life are in the process of a cold and total secularization. It is enough that man be honest, efficient, and socially functioning. Faith, or better whatever one calls faith, is an artificial arrangement of sterilized and blunted "truths" which cause pain to no one and claim to have God at one's disposal. Such a God can, as Orestes expresses in Sartre's *Flies*, be "coasted by" like two ships passing each other, in silence and without greeting.

This indifference which "does not consider itself involved," is far more difficult to cope with than the cold rejection or the hot battles which in former times we considered as afflictions from God. These slick atheists who talk about tolerance can hardly be convinced any longer that "man is only man when he is together with God" (A. Delp).

Remedy: Theology

Here is where the task and service of the theologian begin. First he helps to unmask smiling, progress-enchanted successfulness as a need. He unveils the supposed wealth as a loss of substance and proves that the comfortable ways are actually nothing but anxiety-producing dead-end streets. Then the theologian calls for a new search for God: "God's are those who seek, he lets himself be found" says an old hymn. And "nobody goes so far astray that he cannot find his way back to the fountain which not only allows itself to be found, but even searches for those who are astray and thirsty — never before said about a fountain." So says Kierkegaard, who analyzed our day's anxiety and did not allow himself to consider hope as a hunting dog without a spoor.

As long as hunger and thirst remain in us or are aroused anew, we are on our way to God and God is on the way to us. Only this elementary need for him is necessary. The herdsmen of antiquity used to put salt blocks in the pastures, so that the cattle, by licking them, became thirsty and drank. According to Chrysostom, the words of the theologians should be such salt blocks. Salt blocks of revealed truths should be placed in the playgrounds of man so that, in licking them, he become thirsty for the fountains of life.

The Threefold God, Center of Theological Anthropology

"Man is only man when he is together with God." The image needs a constant confrontation with the original in order to be shaped after it. Anthropology will remain piece-work unless it starts to expand into the dimensions of theology. For divine science is not a quarrel over concepts alien to the world but rather the involvement in life's burning questions. If God is to be the fertile alpha of the image of man, his model and example, then this God cannot be thought of as an abstract, bloodless structure, contrived, "proved" or postulated by philosophers. He who "is beyond all knowledge" is the God of the gospel who reveals himself as Father, Son and Holy Spirit.

Only by reflecting the image of this threefold and triune God can man be truly shaped after him and can God's thought take form within him. Hence it is our concern that the Trinity of God may more and more im-press man who is created after his image.

The book *Father and Fatherhood*[1] I dedicated to meditation on God as Father, trying to render it fruitful for earthly fatherhood — so urgently needed today — whether represented in the father of the family, in the priestly father or in other paternal authorities. Those who deplore today's conception of a harmless and unmanly kind of fatherhood; those who suffer from the relapses into a stern, overdrawn patriarchism, need a new and intensive confrontation with the in-Christ-reconciled Father in heaven. A piety which is content in its Christocentrism fails to see that the Son wants to lead to the Father. In many areas of life we can observe this loss of substance in religious consciousness.

Come Holy Spirit

The Son not only gives witness to the Father, as conversely the Father to the Son, but the Son also gives witness to the Holy Spirit, just as he himself is witnessed by the Holy Spirit. Unfortunately, the relationship of most Christians to the Holy Spirit has shrunk to a minimum of occasional mentions. In the prayer of the primitive Church we can still see very clearly the great line which leads, through the Son in the Holy Spirit, to the Father; but in today's liturgical and private prayer the Holy Spirit (and generally God the Father, too) plays a very secondary, almost unimportant role. In spite of many good attempts and proposals, the meaning of the sacrament of confirmation is not yet fully recognized and appreciated. In a time when socialistic, communistic and liberalistic circles celebrate the adolescent's entrance into life with solemn and pseudo-sacramental rituals, the sacrament of confirmation, which is the anointing by the spirit of witness, is still poorly initiated in most cases, and often unimpressively administered by the Church. Very seldom is this sacred and decisive moment remembered in later years by the confirmed.

Seldom, too, do they pray for the spirit of wisdom and understanding, of counsel and fortitude, of knowledge, piety
and fear of the Lord. Christmas and Easter mean something for the average Christian; but Pentecost — the feast
of the descent of the Spirit, the feast of the foundation of
the Church, the renewal of the face of the world, the feast
of mankind on its way to a general "socialization" — finds
man helpless and unprepared. The great "Veni" of the
primitive Church, the "Come, Lord" of the Christian East,
the expectant openness of the "Orantes" have become almost incomprehensible attitudes. Today's so highly re-
garded prosaicness is as much at a loss with the "flames of
the threefold God" and the "mighty storm of the Spirit of
Love" as the almost neurotic compulsion to act is with the
quietness and the silent waiting for God's action.

In my former work I used the divine Father as a "yardstick" to characterize earthly fatherhood. This book is
dedicated to a similar search into the nature of woman. It
seems to me that there is a profound relationship between
the third divine person, the Holy Spirit, and woman. This
description of the spirit-quality of the woman might then
give new impulse to a theological anthropology and stimu-
late it to see for a change the question of the sexes from
this uncommon and yet, as it seems to me, much needed
viewpoint.

GOD, THE MASCULINE AND THE FEMININE PRINCIPLE

"Et Inhorresco — Et Inardesco"

Even though, as opposed to polytheism and vague pan-
theism, the belief in one God was progress and — in the
case of the Jewish people — a unique accomplishment, we
Christians should not consider our belief in God as a monotheism in the sense of Judaism or Islamism. God is for the

Christian the three times Holy. Therefore we pray in and with the Church: "Not as though you were only one person; you are one only God in three persons." We should not consider the doctrine of the Trinity as a merely insignificant variation of monotheism. "By their fruits you shall know them." Judaism, Islamism and even Calvinism hold a very arid, rationalistic, and in any case very pseudo-masculine concept of God: a consequence of their monotheism. For them, he is, above all, a just, reprimanding and punishing God. God's kindness, tenderness and loveliness are in large part blocked out. Yet, both these sides are mysteriously united in God, even though man cannot completely penetrate and articulate the nature of this union. Thus St. Augustine rightly says: *Et inhorresco — et inardesco,"* at times I recoil in fear and at other times I am drawn by love. The recoil refers to the paternal principle in God, to his authority and power; the burning love and the attraction refer to the maternal principle, to the sheltering, protecting and bestowing God. Here Oda Schneider's[2] phrase comes to our mind: "God is at the same time father and mother" and hence respect and distance as well as loving attraction are the natural reactions of man.

"Androgynous" Primitive Monotheism

Investigations of primitive history and ethnology have pointed out that monotheism was not the end of a long religio-historical evolution but began with the history of mankind. However, this primeval monotheism was certainly not a formal-logical abstract belief but a vital one. How other than as a procreating and life-giving God could men of those days conceive him? Thus recent investigations about primitive man suggest the idea of an "androgynous," that is, a masculine-feminine, monotheism. Accordingly, man, who called God Father, included in this concept the feminine correlate, and when he talked about the *Magna Mater*, the All-Mother, he did not exclude paternal pro-creation. Thus the creator occasionally is represented with breasts and the All-Mother with a beard.

The idea of a supreme deity who is the first principle of both sexes is preserved into historical times. The only thing is that this idea is represented in a primitive sensual way, which, of course, a spiritualized concept of God must reject. Thus the msytery cults which, at the time of Christ, thrived in the entire Eastern mediterranean area and which lasted until the third century, talk about bi-sexual gods. In the Greco-Roman official liturgy Zeus' double-axe and the two-faced Janus give us notions of bi-sexual gods. The divine couples Isis and Osiris in Egypt, Ischthar and Tam-muz in Babylon, Astarte and Adon in Phoenicia, Cybele and Attis in Phrygia and many more among the primitive Finns, the Sibiriacs and the Indians are probably reminis-censes of originally bi-sexual god-ideas, handed down into historical times.

Maternal Traits of God in the Old Testament

Neither is the Old Testament completely untouched by the idea of God being also the feminine principle. In Gen 1:27 it says: "And God created man to his own image; to the image of God he created him. Male and female he created them." As we know, the same Genesis used two different names for God: Yahweh and Elohim. Much guesswork has been done about this second name, Elohim, which is plural, while Yahweh, in most cases, is con-structed as singular. This use of the singular proves that the word Elohim does not in any way imply that polytheis-tic ideas had penetrated into the Old Testament; on the other hand, as far as I can see, up to our day nobody has ever proposed that the plural of the word Elohim might perhaps be a remnant of prehistorical ideas of a masculine-feminine God within Judaism. But would this interpretation be completely devious? Everyone is acquainted with the words of the psalm, so much cited in liturgy (in the newly revised formulation, however, differently translated) (109:3): *"Ex utero ante luciferum genui te"* ("From the womb — uterus — before the day-star I begot thee"). Here there is talk about the womb of God. According to the prophet Isaiah (49:14) the Lord compares himself with a mother. "Sion said, the Lord has forsaken me; my Lord has forgotten me. Can a mother forget her infant, be without tenderness for the child of her womb?" And, according to the same prophet, the Lord asks (66:9): "Shall not I that make others to bring forth children, myself bring forth?" So, here God is spoken of, not as procreator, but one who is giving birth. And finally we might cite the words (66:13) so much used in the liturgy of Advent: "As a mother comforts her son, so will I comfort you, says the Lord." Although the Old Testament is characterized by the idea of a very masculine and stern God, certain recollections of the feminine principle in God have been preserved or, to say it with O. Eberz, have not been able to be completely effaced.

. . . and in the New Testament

In the New Testament, no less a person than John speaks, at the end of his mysterious prologue (1:18), about the "womb of the Father" (in the Vulgate text we read *"sinus"* which primarily means breast). Furthermore, when the Lord calls the promised Holy Spirit "the comforter", we think automatically, once we have heard Isaiah, of a motherly consoling God. Thus one cannot be surprised that Syrian versions, which already in Genesis translate the hovering of the Holy Spirit over the waters with "to breed," call the comforter of the New Testament *"consolatrix."* When Jesus caressed the children, the Holy Spirit seems to have smiled through his face.

The Holy Spirit, Principle of the Feminine

Our reflections on the feminine principle — doubtlessly present and sheltered in God as well as the masculine — led us suddenly into the proximity of the Holy Spirit. Let us pause here to ask whether such considerations are not disrespectful and a shameless, inappropriate contemplation of the mysteries of God. I believe that, while being uncommon, they are not disrespectful. Do we not also hold in esteem medieval theologians, because they worked out and clarified the difference between the generation of the Son and the breathing forth of the Holy Spirit in the threefold life of God? Would not this intellectual accomplishment be equally inappropriate?

However, right here and now let us definitely clarify and underline: when we speak here about the "feminine principle of the threefold God" this is merely a meditation on or better, a consideration of, different manifestations of God under the aspect of the feminine. God's nature and mystery remain untouched and unclarified by this. From the very start let us avoid all gnostic and cabalistic speculations which ascribe a primitive sensual feminine nature to the Holy Spirit. Such notions might be welcome in esoteric circles but they have no place in a level-headed theology of the Holy Spirit.

"In the metaphysics of the triune God, this our mother, the Holy Spirit, did not have the proper place precisely as mother."[3] Theology should see the facing-up to this complaint as one of its central tasks and straightforwardly disclose anew the maternal side of God. As far back as the first Christian centuries we find versions which prove that such thoughts were not uncommon. In the so-called Hebrew gospel,[4] of which we have only a fragment, Christ says: "My mother, the Holy Spirit." This Hebrew gospel does not belong to the canon of inspired writings of the New Testament. It is, to use the theological term, apocryphal. Yet, no less a person than Origen cited this passage in his commentary on John. Moreover the Didascalia, a set of regulations of the Syriac Church in the first decades of the third century, calls the deacon the representative of Christ, and the deaconess the representative of the Holy Spirit — another indication that certain feminine aspects were ascribed to the Holy Spirit. And finally, one might accuse Synesius of Cyrene, the Bishop of Ptolemais between 370 and 375, who sings to God in a hymn, "You are Father, you are Mother" (PL 66, 1493), of gnosticism and neoplatonism. But it is hardly possible to impute any kind of heresy to Clement of Alexandria who was in charge of the Christian catechetical school. This first theologian (about 200 A.D.) expresses the same thought (Paedag. 1:6) when he writes: "God is father and mother, teacher and nourisher."

Eastern Kind of Thinking

Eastern Churches and Christians, with their closer relationship to the Holy Spirit, never allowed this way of thinking to be completely buried. In the icons and paintings of the monks of Athos, the Holy Spirit often takes on a feminine form. We shall not go into details of the Sophia doctrine here. Suffice it to say that also in it such ideas are not unknown. In this context, one might even be tempted to see the apex of Bulgakoff's (who died in 1944, in Paris) sophiological deliberations in the statement: "The Holy Spirit is hypostatized motherliness."[5]

In Germany, Julius Tyciak, among others, wishes to inform the West of this Eastern way of thinking and to render it fruitful for Western theology. He writes[6]: "The Holy Spirit can be called the feminine principle of the Deity, the expression of love, the kiss of the Father and the Son, the overflowing life of God. He is, it could be said, the eternally feminine in its truest form." And in another place: "God is beyond the polarity of the sexes. Yet, in a mysterious way, God is the primary form of the sexes." Likewise, Leon Bloy who, by the way, completely ignored the Greek Church Fathers and who rejected sophiological speculations, saw in the Holy Spirit the "divine principle of the eternally feminine." His pupil Carton called the third divine person "the cosmic virgin."

The Revival of Buried Traditions

Thus, in both East and West, the idea of God as the principle of every origin, the paternal as well as the maternal, is, to some degree, still extant. But the awareness of it is in danger of vanishing. If the feminine sex ever had its own philosophical, religio-sociological and historical tradition at all, it must have been repressed for millenia by paternal cultures, philosophies and theologies. Only in esoteric areas is it lingering. Christian theology, too, is in danger of becoming masculine in form and context. Courage and heroic effort are needed to revive buried traditions and to dig up hidden treasures. "Thus we might say that, on this score, Christendom has to make up for an ancient neglect weighted with consequences. For if not all signs are deceptive, it is the rightful claim of the Great Mother, of nurse and nourisher, as Plato calls her, that gives the neo-pagan movement its elementary and, in its kind, doubtlessly religious impetus — a claim which has been disregarded in Western tradition in spite of Mother Church, the Cosmic Madonna, Devotion to Mary and Crowning of the May Queen. It is a claim which some day could become dangerous for Christendom should it persistently be refused recognition. Let us therefore allow an adequate articulation of the mute reminder which sounds through every gospel passage in which the word pneuma (spirit) is used, and, finally, also in Christian dogma, give to the mother what belongs to the mother! With a commanding gesture she wants, today, to occupy her former place next to the Son and the Father, otherwise she herself will force her re-enthronement in the form of the grossest, most primitive and earthiest manifestations."[7] One thing which does not exist in theology is a *causa finita*, a closed case. Matters of discipline can be settled once and for all by regulations, but theological questions never. For truth is always, at the same time, a gift and a task.

Image of the Nature of God

To constantly encircle the three-sun deity is not only a theological concern but also an anthropological one. Man, by nature a questioning being, questions everything for its own sake and its proper place in the world. But for the great riddle, man, only theology can succeed in finding a solution. Only God can shed light into human darkness. For "man resembles God," says Clement of Alexandria (PG 9:293); and "God resembles man", is the answer given over the centuries to this Father of the Church, by the second Council of Nice. If the Fathers of the East understand theology almost exclusively as a dedication to the mystery of the Trinity, if some centuries were almost shaken by the struggle over trinitarian questions, this is not a sign of withdrawal from the world, or a flight into unworldliness. In the backgound of these theological efforts, there is always simultaneously the question about the nature of man, who is shaped after the image of God. We, the "enlightened clairvoyants" of the twentieth century, can hardly understand why at all times trinitarian heresies have been condemned more severely than other matters subjected to Church discipline. For "being a Christian is the imitation of the nature of God," says Gregory of Nyssa (PG 46:244) and, extending this theology we might say: being a Christian is participation in the threefold life of God. When scholastic theology defines sin as a "turning away from God and towards the creature," this is not to be understood in a moral but in a natural sense. Through sin, man, the copy, separates himself from God, the original. In sinning, man begins a kind of self-fabrication. He denies that he is a copy. Separating himself from God, he makes himself into an idol.

The Woman's Relatedness to the Spirit

In another place (see note 1) we demonstrated that Christian fatherhood can be formed only according to the Christian understanding of the fatherhood of God. Let us hope that a theological meditation on the Holy Spirit will supply important and perhaps even new components for a theology of the woman. Thus, the following chapters will delineate the woman, in three areas, as the spirit-ual being, that is, a being related to the Holy Spirit.

True, Gertrud von Le Fort says "that Catholic dogma has made the greatest statements ever made about woman. Compared with them, all other attempts at a metaphysical explanation of the feminine are but a mere echo of theology or else lack any religious meaning and substance."[8] It is my hope, however, that the presentation of the relationship between the Holy Spirit and woman, and the evidence that the feminine is a bearer of the "spirit" in the trinitarian sense of the word, will add a new dimension and deepen our accepted theological assertions. Here the study of holy scripture no longer leads us to new essential insights. "Biblical texts, after all, have long since been classified . . .

Reduced to itself, exegesis soon touches its frontiers, turns around and marks time, since some of these texts are words spoken merely in passing, without any intention of establishing a theology of the woman. To intend this would mean to violate holy scripture."[9] We know that this is how, in the course of time, an immense literature about woman has come into existence without gaining new viewpoints

Method of Our Train of Thought

In our explanations we shall work by means of analogy. In other words: We believe that a relationship of similarity exists between the Holy Spirit and woman which, notwithstanding the big gap between creator and creature, allows statements that are valid for both. *Woman, in her nature and her functions, resembles the Holy Spirit.* However, not for a single moment can this mean that it would be possible to express the actuality even close to adequately. Our reasoning will always move between the poles: similar — dissimilar. Yet theology feels compelled to talk about God and divine things, well knowing that such talk remains for the most part a mere stammer. Let us try, then, to direct our attention to the spirit-relatedness of the woman, hoping thereby to gain a new insight into her nature.

THE HOLY SPIRIT AND WOMAN ARE ANONYMOUS

Personality, Wrapped in Silence

The personality of the Holy Spirit of God is wrapped in mysterious darkness. Only with great difficulty can it be represented, as the theologians must regretfully confess. Whoever reads only the Old Testament, will actually never know his personality. There the Holy Spirit appears more as a power through which God reveals himself or by which he creates man's supernatural and ethical life. Thus, the Jews, too, understood the spirit of God in no other sense than as an impersonal operative element of Yahweh.

Neither is the reader of the New Testament particularly impressed by the personality of the third divine person. The Greek word "pneuma" is neuter. Time and again we find this neuter article *"to"* (the). Yet it must be noticed, that, in spite of the neuter article, scripture occasionally follows with the masculine. Jesus' order of baptizing, in which he unites the Father, the Son and the Holy Spirit with the equating "and"; also numerous triadic passages of Paul remind us of the personality of this mysteriously veiled pneuma even though no clear evidence is offered. The personality of the Holy Spirit is merely alluded to, is kept secret rather than made public. Only a theological reflection, a systematic "penetration" of the Trinity has "worked out" the personality of the third divine person more clearly than it was given by revelation. And this clarification took place relatively late. Starting with the functions and works attributed to the Holy Spirit and the resulting parallels with Christ, theologians developed a countenance of the Holy Spirit. Great difficulties had to be faced. Also, certain so-called subordinatianist weaknesses, which considered the Holy Spirit inferior to the Father and the Son, could not be avoided. Only Athanasius and the first council of Constantinople (381) smoothed the way for a systematic theology of the Holy Spirit, sowing the seed which sprang up and bore fruit through Augustine (*De Trinitate*) and finally through the theology of Aquinas (S.theol. I, 27,4). The difference between the generation of the Son by the Father and the breathing forth of the Holy Spirit by the Father and the Son, as worked out and articulated by the scholastics in the 13th century, brought the problem of the personality of the Holy Spirit to a sort of conclusion.

Neuter Symbols

It is significant that the individual representation of the Holy Spirit in pictures has always been rare. Since 1745, the Church has allowed the third divine person to be represented only in the form of a dove. But a dove does not give a very strong impression of personality. And so it is that, while the Holy Spirit is the very person in the threefold God in whom God is closest to us men, his countenance has always remained mysteriously veiled to us. We meet his efficacy, praise his fruits (Gal 5:27) and pray for his gifts (Isa 11:2). We see him in the symbol of the "water, coming forth from the throne of God" (Apoc 22:1) and in the gently blowing wind or the roaring storm. We represent him in tongues and fire, giving him impersonal names such as gift, bond and love. Yet, behind all this he himself remains in darkness, practically anonymous. Thus it is understandable that some pneumatologists talk about the revelation of God the Father in the Old Testament, the revelation of the Son in the New Testament and the revelation of the Holy Spirit — whom they extol as the perfect, the golden one — only in a future age.

Anonymity of the Woman

Representing and incorporating God's anonymity on earth is woman. Characteristic of her nature is a certain namelessness. In this she resembles the Holy Spirit. In most countries she loses her maiden name when entering marriage to become the companion of a man and mother of children. From then on she carries the man's name, even after his death. When she solemnly consecrates herself as a virgin to God in order to represent the nuptial mystery of life by her total dedication to him as his bride, she, too, gives away her former name and accepts one that indicates her state of belonging to God. A number of European countries, for reasons of equality, allow women today to keep their maiden names. It is very significant that most of them do not make use of this privilege. They instinctively do not consider bearing their husbands' name a humiliation but an honor which is in accordance with their nature.

As early as in the first chapters of the Old Testament account of creation (Gen 5:2) we meet the anonymous woman. There we read the deeply meaningful words: "As man and woman he created them and called *them* Adam." Both are united with one another in a mysterious unity and bear the name of the man. Up to our day, many European and some Asiatic languages use one and the same word for human being and for male. This is neither a denial of woman's human nature nor a brusque masculine condemnation to namelessness but the expression of an instinctive knowledge of the anonymity of the woman. Concealment and retirement are characteristic of her nature.

The Dignity of Coordination

This is why M. J. Scheeben, the great reviver of Catholic theology, in attempting to sketch a trinitarian picture of marriage,[10] could see the nature of the woman in the dignity of coordination. According to him, the identity-basis of the woman is different from the man's. She understands her "I" only as the one who is called "thou". Hence this almost classical definition of her nature considers the related-ness of woman not as a humiliation and a snub but rather as a specific dignity. If the idea is valid — and theologically it certainly is — that every statement about man has to begin with his being called "thou," then the woman, according to her nature, is closer to this "thou" and thus to the mystery of being man. By nature, she is the "other," she is not word but response, less ray than reflection.

Woman, the Responding Being

This essential characteristic of her nature can be seen in all her relationships. The prefix "re," as everyone knows, means "back." Now, when it comes to the word re-ligion, scholars have different opinions as to the meaning of this syllable — but one thing is certain, that religion contains in both word and fact this "re", this great "back." In this sense the woman is more "religious," since, according to her nature, she responds more easily to the thou-calling God. In marriage, too, the woman is not the one who speaks first but the one who re-sponds. The word is man's due, re-sponse the woman's. And finally the woman is associated in a special way with helping the needy, with weakness and human misery. These, then, are the three relationships of woman: she is "towards" God, "towards" her marital companion, "towards" the children and any kind of need. In her total relationship to God she is virgin. As the natural completion of the man, she is bride and companion. As the life-giving and sheltering one she is mother. In these three fundamental relationships let us try to paraphrase the nature of woman under the total aspect of an analogy of the Holy Spirit.

The Veil, Symbol of Coordination

The symbol of coordination, the symbolic expression of a state of belonging, is the veil. It wards off shameless obtrusion from the outside and indicates the limits of reserve that are to be held by everyone external to this woman's relationship. Moreover, through its seclusion and discretion, the veil gives shelter to the mystery of a two-in-oneness, in which woman is anonymous in her dedication to God, to the man or to the child. It would be foolish, however, to confuse this kind of namelessness of the woman with the anonymity of the human mass, with the facelessness and irresponsibility of a collective particle or of the impersonal "one" as expressed in cultivated contemporary usage. The veil both protects and shelters a face which is turned towards God or the man. It is the chaste reminder of the bearer's relatedness, of her state of belonging. It prohibits every isolated way of thinking about the woman and outlines the big "and" which unites the woman with God, with the man and with life. The man, for reasons of method or of an efficient mastery of the world, may separate again and again; but attached to woman's veil is the reminder of the nuptial mystery of every life, the blush that followed the loss of original union and the nostalgia for a restoration of the happiness of a paradisaical union in a future golden age. And so the veil is, at one and the same time, a historical reminder and a prophetical indication. From this it becomes clear how the striving for emancipation and equality can easily and erroneously isolate the woman, and with cold-eyed view and pointed emphasis on her individuality, completely fail to understand the relatedness of her nature. The result is — while thinking that you are serving woman — you are destroying her. The veil which civilized eyes do not see, or rudely want to do away with, prevents the woman from being thought of in the isolated way in which we can consider the man.

The Veil of Betrothal to God

Thus the veil expresses coordination, relatedness and belonging. First, *relatedness to God*. Going back to the Romans, we already find the veil of the Vestal virgin a reminder of her bethrothal to God. But here relatedness was only temporary. After some years the vestal virgin was set free from her unconditional relationship to God. The Christian virgin consecrated to God gives him her entire life. She is wedded to him and carries therefore the ring of lifelong fidelity. The wonderful ritual of the consecration of a virgin states at the moment of giving her the veil: "Receive the holy veil as a sign that you despise the world and have surrendered truly and humbly with all the striving of your heart to be the bride of Christ for ever." After receiving the veil, the consecrated virgin sings immediately: "a seal he has put upon my face that I may accept no lover but him alone." The symbolism of act and words is clear. Just as the married woman wears the veil as a sign of her dedication to the one man who alone is allowed to lift the veil and gaze upon her face, so the virgin wears the veil because she is the property of the Lord and wants to remain concealed from the world. Tertullian already explained the veil of the virgin in this manner when he wrote (*De virg. vel.* Chap. 16): "Indeed you are truly married: you have espoused yourself to Christ." Thus, through all ages, Christian art has represented Mary, the one who belonged totally to God, with the veil as a sign of this relatedness to God.

Apocalyptic Strip-Tease

Conversely the removal or deliberate discarding of the veil is a terrible and abominable sign of a divorce from God. This is the awesome symbolism of the 12th chapter of the Apocalypse, in which the woman, the great whore, the incorporation of all godlessness, tears up her veil in an apocalytic strip-tease. In doing so she not only shows her nakedness and vanity. The tearing of the veil is not just an expression of immorality, as for instance, are terrible violations of the sixth or ninth commandment. It is much more. It is the symbolic expression of an absolute getting rid of God. It is as if the world would fling the ring of fidelity before God's feet. The world refuses to belong; it wants to be independent and to hang on to its own right. With this the godless world sits in judgment upon itself. It has stripped itself not only in the moral but also in the literal sense of the word. The cosmic whore tearing her veil is the pitiful expression of the diabolical *"non serviam"* which can also mean "I do not want to belong."

The veil, then, indicates the relationship of the woman to her husband. According to the customs of ancient Rome, the woman was given the red *flammeum* as a sign of her marriage. Using the term *nubere* (to conceal, to veil), women were called *nuptae*, that is, those who are veiled. The wedding was called *nuptiae*. The festive fiery-red combined with the saffron-yellow of the veil was the lifelong identification of the married woman. In the Orient, too, long before Mohammed, married women were veiled. As early as in Genesis 24:6, we see Rebecca taking the veil at the moment when, for the first time, she saw Isaac, her future husband. Paul, in Cor 11:7, was, after all, not making innovations but merely insisting upon established traditions when he advised women to use the veil. "She is, after all, (merely) the reflection of man."

The converse is the case when the wife or the virgin who belongs to God is violently deveiled. Through all of Europa and Asia, this is a sign of absolute dishonor. According to Dan 13:32, Susanna, supposedly caught in the act of adultery, was made to remove her veil — a common custom before stoning an adulteress. And, since not only in the field of art, but also in popular opinion, woman's long hair could replace the veil, Paul considers cutting the hair of the woman a sign of dishonor. Even in our day, we find in many places the custom of forcibly cutting the hair of an adulteress in order to make her disgrace known. This is the same as tearing off the veil.

The Universal Discovery of the Woman

It is symptomatic of our time that everywhere the veil

is disappearing. Even in Mohammedan countries it is losing its meaning — among certain groups of educated women or in entire countries, so as Turkey, it has completely disappeared. The fashions of European and American women are changing rapidly, but with one thing in common — to dis-cover rather than to veil the woman. This indicates more than a mere change of taste. The dis-covery of the woman shows visibly that modern man regards woman as unbound. While other periods saw the ideal of woman represented as virgin or as companion and helper of the man; while former times were oriented towards the rural woman in care of the household and farm, or the middle-class woman and mother of many children; the idol of our day seems to be more and more the unmarried woman free in every sense and pursuing some kind of nonpersonal occupation. The "stars" magically painted on the teenager's heaven by the dream-producing movie industry are women who are not committed to anybody or anything, who no longer feel themselves bound. These stars want anything but the veil, they want to be put on a pedestal and be in the public eye. It would be so simple to say that the veil is merely one of the many symbols lost by twentieth century man. But it seems to me that this has a deeper meaning. Together with the veil was lost the relatedness of the woman. If this is true the missing veil in contemporary woman's fashions is the revelation of that loss.

Being Beautiful for . . .

Such being the case, a mere reestablishment of the veil or pleading for its cause would serve little or no purpose. It is not a question of eliminating the symptoms, but of curing the ailment itself. This requires an insight into its mysterious depth. Men and women must once more be convinced of the nature-preserving value of the veil, then modifications in forms of living and everyday behavior will be an automatic consequence. Here we are not thinking so much of the exterior but the interior veil. Woman must once more recognize her relatedness and give evidence of it in everyday life and expression. Our meaning can easily be illustrated by the example of cosmetics. St. Thomas already answered this question in our sense. He says that cosmetics for women are allowed not just to conceal an illness or something ugly, but *"ut placeant viris suis"* (that they may please their husbands). Of course the woman is allowed to make herself beautiful; this is her privilege and is an extension of her nature. But she should beautify and adorn herself *for him*, her bridegroom, her husband . . . not for everybody. What bothers us in many a woman's glamorous face is the erotic everyman program pursued with every trick and dodge, this obtrusion upon men which is so incongruous with true womanliness. Whoever sees and experiences the impact of this wanton art of seduction, to which man is exposed in streets, offices and factories, will, consequently, be strongly inclined to turn the mere concurrence in the use of cosmetics, given by the great teacher of the Church seven hundred years ago, into a precept for married women. The way the woman's face is made up should once more make man aware of the veil, the sign of her relatedness.

The Veil Envelops the Two-in-oneness

The relationships between man and woman today require the veil in another respect. In various countries it is customary in the marriage ceremony to put the woman's veil around the man's shoulders, too. Since they are united from now on in a holy two-in-oneness, the veil is meant to suggest the sphere of intimacy which envelops both, and the necessity of its preservation. Certain impenetrable barriers of reserve surround their shared secrets and guard their silence. And it is quite meaningful that the veil belonging to the woman is given to the man. The man's drive tends outward, wants to make things public. Therefore, the man is easily tempted to show off his possession and boast about the beauty of his wife. Like King Candaules men are inclined to display their wives and share secrets. The primitives organize potlatches, that is, bragging contests; modern men, in order to demonstrate and emphasize their social status, set great value in flashy cars and squander a fortune on overloading their wives with jewels and luxuries. This behavior is not so much an expression of love as it is a gloating provocation of potential competitors, and a self-complacent pride over the fact that the man is the sole owner and the sole favorite of this concoction he calls his woman. The natural veil within the woman's heart must find such exhibition unbearable and this is precisely why the external veil, the symbol of the threshold, is put around the shoulders of *both* during the wedding ceremony. The true woman guards the shared mystery of life from publicity. Every third person is an outsider and without authorization. At the same time the fertile tension within the two-in-oneness is preserved since each one faces only the other.

Star Cult vs. Anonymity

"The veil, in fact, is the credential of every great feminine mission" (Le Fort). It is only the woman who can preserve the veil and thus help to rediscover the necessity and value of the sphere of intimacy. True, modern man does not think much of names concealed by the veil of anonymity. Quite the contrary. Names are directly challenged, pampered and artificially cultivated. The widespread star cult is a striking example. The star is anything but humble.

Unscrupulously she takes advantage of every possible opportunity to use the people around her for her own purpose. The result of this is characteristic: instead of a truly human communication, we find a kind of isolation which the star foolishly considers of greater value but which in fact is the sign of a cold loss of contact. But twentieth century man, and especially the young, should recognize that "kooky" manners, calculated caprice and deliberatedly provoked scandals are not the expression of a refined way of life, even when millions ape these ways — which is probably the very intention of the promoters. Such antics may be appropriate means to gain publicity — and with the publicity a high and entirely disproportionate remuneration; but publicity is not yet a sign of greatness.

Protection Against Publicity

Lucifer, the "light-bearer," even promised Adam and Eve that their "eyes would be opened." Thus he talked disillusionment already to our first parents and was successful with his device: "see things as they really are." There is, indeed, something luciferous in the urge to publicize what ought to be reverently guarded and which preserves its authentic value only when concealed. What a dubious source of pride for *homo technicus* when, by using highly sensitive microphones, he succeeds in listening in on his fellow man hundreds of yards away! What a hatred of man it really is to uncover through so-called lie-detectors what a person would have preferred to be kept secret, and use every device to penetrate shamelessly into the intimate sphere of one's home or life. Our first parents' eyes were opened in a way they had never suspected. The eyes of the advocates of a totally X-rayed life, will also not only be opened but they will bulge out. They promise a greater experience of reality, but sooner or later they will have to realize that things and men withdraw from them for they cannot exist without veil.

Modern Striptease Dances

It is not meaningless that pampered stars who constantly celebrate the cult of their names readily favor the widespread urge for publicity and practice intellectual and phy, sical exhibitionism with almost perverse dedication. For even published diaries and written memoirs have often but the one goal: showing off. Furthermore these strip-teases are performed before the eyes of a voracious public at an age when a normal human being is just beginning his real life, and are motivated and inspired by actions and behavior contradictory to true life. The strip-tease exhibitions in the soulless and, in the deepest sense, deserted (that is, devoid of true humanity) night clubs of our big cities which glorify unveiling as "art" and pay high prices for it, are merely a physical expression of the equally popular and far more dangerous spiritual strip-teases constantly "celebrated" before the eyes of a gaping public.

According to depth psychologists, the urge to show off often stems from frustrated inferiority complexes. If this is correct — and there is, it seems to me, much truth behind it — then the frequent and highly favored physical and literary strip-teases indicate that behind the smiling mask of self-possession is hidden a full measure of insecurity and need of protection. Deep down, next door to the radiant recklessness, may be the sense of emptiness and worthlessness. For at all times man has fenced in and guarded what is valuable and sacred, awesome and sublime, trying to preserve it by definitely regulated, yet changing, arcana. Violators of this modesty have always been punished since they profaned and secularized cultic values and thus, together with the cultic values, jeopardized culture itself. It was left to our time not only to fail to punish those offenders but even to decorate and honor the violators of modesty and the gravediggers of culture skilled in technique and shamelessness.

No Culture Without Veil

As a matter of fact, culture is impossible without the veil. With no veil, masculine enlightening, clarifying and grasping might make things practicable and manipulative but this is not yet culture. Man feels compelled to test his energies on the world and to transform them into visible works. He wants to make a name for himself. He is like the inhabitants of Babel who also according to Genesis 11:4, began to build their heaven-aspiring tower with the words: "Let us make a name for ourselves." Hence the building of the Babylonian tower proved to be a typically civilizational but not a cultural achievement. For not the least important difference between culture and civilization is that civilization clarifies, enlightens and tries to make understandable and accessible that which culture protects against the desecrating grip of curious *ratio*. True culture, therefore, has always included a full measure of anonymity and silence about names and has cherished respect for the mystery of the creation as well as for its creator, while our times advocate almost the reverse, ambition for profanation.

A woman entirely swept up in the wake of masculinity, inevitably will find it impossible to recognize and fulfill her great task of restoring culture in the sign of the veil. Only when she, reflecting back on her nature, succeeds in disillusioning those who exuberantly celebrate their own enlightenment, can she make the contribution expected from her — which only she can make — that it is necessary to be aware that many a progress is a setback and many a regression is true progress. Her service would then be truly a "revolution" — in the original sense of the word — a folding back. For this very masculine faith in progress has to be convinced once more that the barbarian is not the product of the beginning of man's history but rather of its end, when his power and knowledge are augmented merely by the skills of publication and destructive techniques. A sense of dignity and value and a new security can grow only under the protection of the veil which has to be discovered anew. The woman who, like the Holy Spirit, is anonymous, related and veiled, owes it to our times to give evidence of this.

Chapter 2

THE HOLY SPIRIT
AND THE WOMAN
ARE RECEIVERS

THE RESPONDERS

The Holy Spirit, The Receiver

To start with, some of the medieval teaching of the Trinity, for instance that of Thomas Aquinas, must be introduced. The scholastics speak about active and passive principles in the threefold life of God. The two principles constituting God's fatherhood are active. He generates the Son and together with the Son breathes forth the Holy Spirit. Sonship consists in an active and a passive principle. The Son is generated by the Father but together with the Father breathes forth the Holy Spirit. The Holy Spirit is entirely passive, the one who is breathed forth by the Father and the Son. His personality consists in having-received.*

Theologians emphasize explicitly that the breathing forth of the Holy Spirit differs essentially from the generation of the Son and, therefore, they speak very consciously about a coming forth. According to Thomas, the Holy Spirit can

* Of course, we cannot understand these relations of the three divine persons in any kind of temporal sequence. God is eternal not only according to his nature but also in his relations which constitute the persons. Thus the third divine person is equally eternal and worthy of adoration. He is the eternal breath of love between the Father and the Son.

be truly called "donum", that is, gift (I,38:2). Therefore, among the divine persons, it is his special lot to be passed on as gift (C. Gent 4:23). Within the threefold life of God, the Holy Spirit is in no sense word, but the eternal and great response. J. Tyciak, whom we mentioned above, now becomes more understandable (see note 6) when he calls the Holy Spirit the "kiss" of the Father and the Son and sees in this kiss the eternal feminine in its purest form.

The Coming Forth of Eve

We have already mentioned the definition of J. M. Scheeben, who sees woman's dignity in coordination. In this context the great theologian points out that the first book of Moses presents Eve's creation as an analogy of the coming forth of the Holy Spirit as seen by the theologians. For also when referring to Eve, we speak not of a creation but of a coming forth from the side of Adam. It is very significant that we find no parallel to this in non-biblical traditions. Eve and the Holy Spirit have "come forth." Paul, too (1 Cor 11:7-9), presumably is thinking of the special nature of Eve's coming forth when he calls the woman a reflection or glory of man and, because of her origin, orders her to keep her veil. Methodius of Olympus, a Greek Church writer of the late third century, even takes the liberty to call Eve *costa Verbi*, that is, the side, or the rib of the word. Christ and Adam are word, the Holy Spirit and Eve are response.

The Woman, Vas Spirituale

Thus, the first statement about the woman will have to be that, according to her nature, she is the one who receives. If we should try to express this fundamental principle of her nature by means of a geometric figure, it could be done only by depicting a chalice-like, open half-circle. The chalice has the form of receiving and taking in. Its purpose is to be filled. We invoke Mary, the renewal and embodiment of true femininity, in the litany as *vas spirituale,* as spiritual vessel. Her *"fiat"* is a valid expression of this chalice-like openness and readiness. In this one word, all created being is incorporated before God. Mankind, in need of salvation, unconditionally surrenders to its Lord. While the woman assumes this readiness and openness by virtue of her nature, it is a difficult struggle for the man to force his heart, which is "bent back towards himself" (Augustine), into a truly religious attitude. In other words, the unspoiled woman is related to and open for God by her very nature, the man only through moral effort. It then follows: "Whenever a woman is herself, at her very depths, she is not herself but dedicated to whatever she dedicates herself. There she is also bride and mother" (Le Fort) and this also means: the companion of man. In conclusion we might state once more that the coordination and the "belonging" of the woman express a dignity and not a defect or devaluation. This, however, is a specifically Christian evaluation.

The Consequences of Dualistic Thinking

Pagan Matter Form Thinking

Pagan antiquity's extremely masculine way of thinking could not understand the concept of dedication and belonging. Its pure dualism tends to evaluate the one principle as positive and the other as negative. Everything active is positive: intellect, form, light; in short, everything masculine. The passive is negative: matter, darkness, the worldly; in short, woman. Unformed matter requires form for its full existence. Only the form is good. Matter is evil. Matter is characterized as something unordered, chaotic, something which lacks spirit. Thus the body, too, is something inferior, something to be ashamed of, or even to be freed from. (Suicide is a virtue, and, among philosophers, almost epidemic). The woman, so deeply related to the physical and the sexual, is, of course, quickly swept up in the wake of this devaluation of body and sexuality. "The good principle created light and man; the bad created darkness and woman" is a Pythagorean axiom. Plato praises the gods for making him free and a man, and with this "praise of God" he is in the company of all male Jews who sang such praise almost daily to Yahweh. Aristotle, investigating the question of the real nature of the feminine, apparently was willing to acknowledge only the man as a human being: "The feminine is feminine because it lacks some essential qualities."

Dualistic Infiltration into Christendom

Two forms of this dualistic thinking penetrated into Christianity, which, considering its sources, should really have drawn much healthier conclusions. One was neoplatonism and the morally very strict, almost heroic stoicism. Poorly understood Christian teaching sometimes identified itself and sometimes competed with it and at times even tried to outdo its apathetic virtuousness. This was ordinarily an unconscious and semi-official procedure. The other way was a more or less official adoption of Aristotelian doctrine by medieval scholastics. But Aristotle was a dualist. Thus, with the adoption of his system of thought, the foundations of a "good" part of the devaluation of matter and an underevaluation of woman was laid, which the Christian superstructure never has been able to completely counterbalance.

Antagonism to Culture and Woman

Here are a few "fruits" of this infiltration and adoption

which time and again we Christians — not quite unjustly — have been blamed for. Even though in our twentieth century no theologian would approve of these formulations and practice in the crass sense of the term, we should not be unaware of the fact that behind many a "religious" statement, many disguised tensions and obvious failures is an education which has never completely overcome the old pagan dualism. Tertullian calls the woman "the gate of hell." For him, she seems to be the fishing pole used by the devil to cause man's fall. By her very nature, woman is a constant danger. Clement of Alexandria thinks every woman should blush at the thought of her womanhood. He, otherwise so sensible and meritorious a theologian and a truly great light in divine science, has no understanding of the personal value of woman. For him, her passivity is a defect and, in a natural not in a moral sense, is evil. The ascetics of the desert put flight from the world, antagonism to culture and antagonism to woman in one package. Their attitude led them into such devious anti-sexual acrobatics (*virgines subintroductae*) that they slept at night with beautiful women in the same bed to prove both to these virgins and the surprised world that, out of contempt for their sex, they would not touch them. The Knights of the Cross who forced their wives who remained at home to wear the chastity belt, had basically the same mentality in this dishonorable treatment — that is, the idea that woman tends toward evil by nature. Or just recall the story about St. Geneveve of Brabant. The man does not even investigate the false accusations. They must be true; the accused is a woman.

"And see, it was very good!"

The unique magnificence of our account of creation is seen in the fact that, instead of reverting to the dualistic representations of the environment, which certainly were well-known, it sees everything, including matter, flesh and woman, as created by the hands of God. "And see, it was very good" (Gen 1:31). We know, of course, that Genesis is neither a textbook of natural science nor a history of civilization; it offers in imagery a religious view of man's basic nature. Yet, in this very context the pictures chosen convey such strong impressions and wholesome beauty that they rule out per se the possibility of negative implication in any created being.

The Masculine Old Testament

True, the first book of Moses differs greatly from the rest of the Old Testament. In the first place, nonbiblical dualisms seem to have crept into the originally positive concept of the relationship between the sexes, and secondly, the Jewish attitude towards this question came to be more and more derived from a purely masculine, if not pseudo-masculine, prespective. Their extremely masculine concept of God was certainly an important factor. For instance, a very complicated system of greeting came into existence which minutely regulated who had to greet whom, when and where. The woman was excluded from this regulation; she was not greeted at all. Adultery on her part was severely punished while there was little or none for the man. There is no word about companionship! She finds herself accepted only as a mother of numerous children, but above all, of sons. She is supposed to slave from morning till evening while the man sits at the gate boasting about her the way a farmer does about a good plow-horse (Prov 31:10-31). The single state is not considered a worthwhile status; virginity is merely a transitional state to marriage and motherhood. Thus, Jephte's daughter does not bewail her terrible death as the victim of her father's human sacrifice, but her unfulfilled life as a virgin. Except for Genesis, the entire Old Testament manifests the hard, masculine character of grasping and possessing. The law is masculine, the prophets are masculine, David's psalms, the miracles of Moses and the fasting of Elias are masculine. So is the odor of the sacrificial hecatombs offered in the temple.

THE HOUR OF THE COMMITTED

"Porta Coeli"

In the New Testament the exploiters have clearly lost out. Now the cosmic hour of the committed has dawned, the celestial hour of those open for God. The very masculine John who reaches from the Old into the New Testament might be "the greatest among those born of woman," yet "the least in the kingdom of heaven is greater than he". (Matt 11:11). The virgin, described in tender words, is *"porta coeli,"* the gate of heaven on earth. Virginal openness and dedication, as a distinctive quality of human nature, is the complementary counterpart of the generating, creating fatherhood of God. And so the virgin becomes the place of God's presence on earth. Her life is witness to God's right of total possession and, at the same time, she makes evident the feminine principle in absolute purity and inviolateness. This feminine principle is the principle that all creatures belong to and are dedicated to God. Marco Polo, the Venetian merchant, who as early as the thirteenth century had travelled to Peking, observed that it was customary among the Tibetans not to marry a virgin. A great awe kept them from marrying one who belonged totally to God. Thus it becomes understandable that many nations of antiquity considered the violation of virginity as adultery since this act destroyed union with God. Among the vestal virgins, "adultery" was even punished with death, since by their virginal life they represented the nation as belonging to God.

Lopsided View of Productiveness

The ancients knew (what today needs urgently to be recalled to mind) that the virgin is the purest and most valid form of femininity. Times of extreme biologism and exclusively worldly thinking cannot understand this. No wonder that national-socialism called the virgin a "biological zero." Since she has no place in the pseudo-mystical context of "blood and soil" and since she gives birth neither to workers nor to soldiers for the state she was considered unproductive; for productiveness is measured merely according to biological standards and socio-political viewpoints. In the same manner, bolshevism wants to force upon every woman the concept of politically useful productivity. An honest check of our everyday language and of the opinions and advice of many parents will show, unfortunately, that their private deliberations are not far removed from the biological speculations of national-socialism and the political attitude of communism. In German for example, the unmarried woman is addressed by the diminutive *"Fräulein"* as though she, the unmarried, has not reached the full maturity of the woman. It is true that recently any unmarried woman over 30 can insist on being addressed as Frau (Mrs.), but if this should mean that she considers her virginity something negative — a shortcoming — she would herself confirm this widespread error. Likewise we should correct the manner and tone of those well-meaning mothers who want to save their adolescent daughters from the "ignominy" of being "left on the shelf" and who think that the only fulfillment of womanhood is marriage. Henri de Montherlant, who labels a woman dwarfed if she is of no use to the man, would thoroughly enjoy the advice and concern of such mothers.

Fertility through Undividedness

Virginity is neither stunted femininity nor sterility. It is rather the highest kind of fertility which springs from a complete dedication to God. It is like the fertility of the Trinity itself, which also consists in the undividedness of mutual dedication. Gregory Nazianzen (PG 36:144) means this when he says: *"Prima Virgo est Beata Trias,"* the first virgin is the Holy Trinity. This is a supernatural fertility, however, inaccessible to one who thinks on a merely natural level. For, natural fertility originates in sexual dividedness in which the vertical line going from God to man is intercepted by a horizontal line. But supernatural fertility is entirely vertical and springs from an undivided total dedication of virginal humanity open to God.

Enhancement of the Ability to Love

Will not this total dedication to God destroy something of the original and humanly natural ability to love? The "wisdom" of the man on the street answers "yes", generalizing about the failures of the unmarried. But to be an unmarried woman does not yet mean to be a virgin in the sense described here. To conclude in this way, from unhappy forms of unmarried life, that sexual abstinence is unnatural and abnormal and that virginity leads to physical and psychological illness is therefore too simple. In fact, modern science has a completely different opinion. Psychologists speak of possible and quite legitimate equivalents of the sexual life, and refer to artistic, scientific and social activities. They maintain that, while something of the original and natural capacity to love is always lost through such equivalents, this does not hold for the highest form of sublimation, the total dedication to God. The one who dedicates all his capacities, including the sexual — and this above all — to a transcendent goal, will not only avoid this loss of capacity to love but even increase it. Thousands of nuns in the leprosaria of our missions, thousands who, in loving devotedness, alleviate the physical and psychological misery of those around them, are living proofs of our scientists' thesis. Such sublimations are, to use the technical term, "the equivalent of fulfillment."

The Body, Put Into Service

Theologians have all too often maintained that Eros, the love enkindled by fellow man, and Agape, the divine love originating in God, exclude one another. When speaking of virginity, they are easily tempted to quote from the numerous treatises on this subject mushrooming in the fourth century, unaware that they were intended to be a defense against a general nadir of morals, particularly in sexual life. Virginity, therefore, was praised not so much as an abstention "for the sake of the kingdom of heaven" but rather as a renunciation or even denial of sexual life in general. The general immorality of this period simply led to a tense narrowing of view. The wonderful name, virginity, was used for a hasty flight into a very narrowly interpreted negative chastity, which, to give one example, could no longer see the sacramental graces of marriage. Virginity became confused with abstinence for its own sake and with a devaluation of everything sexual. This was accompanied by a proud hostility against the body which corresponded neither to the spirit of Holy Scripture nor to the original doctrine. Virginity, however, is not a victory over the body but puts the body into service. The unaffectedness of St. Hildegard of Bingen, the openness with which she speaks about the physical and the sexual, could set us right on this subject. Whoever exposes himself totally to the light of God will continue to radiate. Virginity, thus, cannot be stuffy, muggy narrowness but must be singing, and a life-accepting joy rooted in God. To make this evident is the task of both theologians and virgins. And this means that the theologians should either get rid of these fourth-century treatises, or else call them what they really are: a denial of the sex prescribed by the times. And the virgins should free themselves of everything prudish and negative in their style of clothing and way of acting. (see Pius XII's exhortation on changing the nuns' garb).

Rejection of the Mysticism of the Bride

Luther, too, could not see virginity, and preferred marriage. Except for the positive approach of the Marian Sisters of Darmstadt and Grandchamp, which bears no weight, modern Protestantism still displays the same attitude. Karl Barth and Emil Brunner reject the so-called mysticism of the bride in any form. According to them, love for God is the "love of the soul which has sinned before its Lord;" but this love could never be the love of a bride for her bridegroom; that, if you do not take into consideration the basic nature of sin, the relationship between God and the soul is a dangerous short circuit, and that grace, therefore, is always only mercifulness of God. Since this way of thinking no longer finds any trace of salvation in man's fallen state, it fails to see that true virginity is, so to speak, the afterglow of a paradise never completely lost, that it is reminiscent of and pointing toward a state beyond sin. Here becomes apparent the great gap sin opened up between God and man, according to the Protestant concept. Yet, there is, it might be noted, an Evangelical community of monks in Taizé, France, which is again adhering to virginity "because of a greater availableness to God, unconditional and irrevocable, comparable to an indissoluble marriage" (M. Thurian).

Loss of Paradise

When we look back at the story of Eden, the devil's attempt to effect apostasy from God through Eve seems to be not so much a flanking movement — as often represented — but rather a frontal attack. Time and again theologians have maintained that the devil addressed Eve because he suspected that she was the weaker part of mankind. Thus Thomas Aquinas (II,II:165) says: *"mulier erat infirmior viro, unde magis seduci poterat,"* the woman was the weaker and thus could be seduced more easily. This opinion originates in the already mentioned basic attitude that woman by nature is more inclined to evil. A very proud masculine opinion — for actually the contrary seems to be true. The devil does not mince matters. In Eve, he makes a direct attack upon the most powerful religious principle of creation: her womanhood, her belongingness to God, her virginity. Once Eve is conquered, Adam is obviously no longer a problem. With laconic brevity it is stated: "She gave some to her husband and he ate" (Gen 3:6). After the devilishly skillful victory over the woman, the man's sin seems to be the easily achievable consequence of the principal rejection of God by Eve.

Its Afterglow

In our post-paradisaical world, virginity remained an afterglow of man's original and actual belongingness to God. As long as this undivided devotion to God is being lived in the world, paradise is never completely lost. Just as the evening glow keeps alive for a long time the remembrance of a wonderful day, so the virgin reminds us of the necessity and possibility of being free for God. The *virgo* is the living question to her fellow man: How much of paradise is still within you? Only God knows how many times the fear of being reminded of this hides behind the mockery and contempt of virginity. The virgin touches the wound of God in man.

The Prophetical Dawn

But the virgin's function is not merely to be a reminder. According to the New Testament, the office of prophecy is also proper to her nature. The virgin is, so to speak, an eschatological sign, a living indication of the dawning final day. Woven through the entire New Testament is the notion that, for the present, God's people are only engaged to Christ, while the wedding is still to come. Jesus calls himself the bridegroom (Matt 9:15; 25:1-10; Mark 2:19-20; Luke 5:34-35). The marriage feast will still take place (Matt 22:1-14). The primitive Church continues to speak in this manner. Paul (Eph 5:32) talks about marriage as a "mystery." Speaking prophetically of the expected marriage with Christ the bridegroom, he uses the biblical term "to know" to designate the marital union: we shall "know" as we are "known." In this world the virgin is at once still undivided — and *already* undivided. She follows "the Lamb wherever he goes" (Apoc 14:4) and therefore is among "those who were purchased from among men, first-fruits unto God" (Apoc 14:4). The enlightened singer of the psalms already saw the wedding procession of those first-fruits "enter the palace of the king" (Ps 45:16). When Our Lord prophesies that the saints in heaven "neither marry nor are given in marriage" (Matt 22:30; Mark 12:25), he is referring to this angelic undividedness of their belonging to God. In marital life man is "divided" (1 Cor 7:34), but the time will come when the original state of an undivided belongingness to God will be re-established. The virgin, already here and now, points to this future state. Her undividedness is a fore-taste of the eternal wedding feast, of the "knowing" of God and the "being known" by God, where God will be all in all and completely sufficient.

Virginal Witness

That the vessel of belonging-to-God may become more and more perfect, all slag of worldliness must be burned up. The virgin, too, is flesh and blood. In her members, too, the power of sin is not broken. On her soul, too, press down the weights of this world. Her heart, too, will never completely overcome the danger of bending back on itself. But what distinguishes her from others is the courage to give herself completely to the purifying and refining fire of the Holy Spirit. She is the very one who experiences that God's love can be not only tender but also painful. Only when every tie to this world is burned away in the ascending divine fire, can she "be saved, yet so as through fire" (1 Cor 3:15). Virginity, therefore, as an important kind of witness, is not much different from the witness of martyrdom. What the martyr testifies by blood and by offering his bodily life, the virgin professes in her living. God has cured her deafness: she has learned to hear and her whole life is a listening to God. She burns every interference to the love of the Holy Spirit. Thus she strives not only to *give* response to God but to *be* the response-made-flesh. She does this through the Holy Spirit who is himself the love-response within the trinitarian love-conversation between the Father and the Son. Thus the early Church rightly spoke of two kinds of martyrdom, the red and the white, that is, the witness of the blood and the crystal clear witness of the virgin.

Creation, Not Cosmos

Natural scientists like to refer to the world as cosmos. This designation calls attention to the system of laws which governs it, and which they investigate and admire. It is, of course, the right term for a world where everything is "ordered by measure, number and weight." But when "cosmos" implies simultaneously the idea of a fundamentally finished, isolated world, there is danger of becoming deaf to God who is unceasingly speaking into it, and insensitive to man's need of constantly communicating with his creator. A world which considers itself an "isolated society" has no antenna to receive God's wooing of love, his call and his summons to service. The Christian interpretation of the world prefers, therefore, the term "creation" to "cosmos." Creation is also like a chalice, opening upwards, expressing a perpetual readiness for being fulfilled. At the beginning of the Old Testament, God pours himself into his creation in the streams of the Holy Spirit. At the beginning of the New Testament, the same Spirit of God hovers over the Virgin. Gertrud von Le Fort's expression that Mary is "the dedicating power of the cosmos" can be understood only in the sense that in her the sinful crust of self-centeredness has been finally burst and so the cosmos becomes a creation into which God's generating love pours once again. With Mary's "fiat" the cosmos abandons its self-willed life of pure lawfulness and effects the salvific move towards the great *communio* with God. The diabolic circle, closed within itself, opens into a *vas spirituale,* a vessel of the Holy Spirit. The people of the Old Testament see themselves represented in the man — in Abraham and Jacob, for example — who by nature finds it harder to be open. But in the New Testament the woman, or, more exactly, the virgin, is the symbol of God's people (see 2 Cor 11:2; Eph 5:27; Apoc 12:1-6; 21:2,9; 22:17). Through the image of the virgin, new mankind gives itself to God who alone works eternal salvation.

Every Soul: The Bride of God

Need it be expressly mentioned that, aside from the characteristically feminine power, the man, too, is called upon to put this into realization in his life? The Latin word for virgin, *virgo,* is derived from *vir,* the man. Although such a conception might have been alien to the pagan Romans, we Christians interpret these terms in the sense that both these forms of human existence are profoundly related, and think that the relationship consists in the "belonging to God." "*Ad duas Virgines*" — "to the two virgins" was the title occasionally given to churches in the Middle Ages, alluding to Mary and John, "who rested on the heart of the Lord." Hence we are not surprised to hear from Origen that in many places, during the first Christian centuries, the ascetics wore a veil. And we know that the monks of certain Oriental rites still wear it today. Thus the veil is a sign that every man and woman is the virginal bride of God — all "who are eunuchs for the sake of the kingdom of heaven" (Matt 19:12).

"Every soul can become the bride of the eternal Word," we read in the Cherubian Wanderer. Actually it should say: "every soul *must*" — even the soul of the man. Only, the man who experiences grasping and possessing to be more proper to his nature, is bound to have much more difficulty in finding his way towards a virginal openness-to-God. The unmarried man will have it somewhat easier than the married. Nevertheless, even the married man must learn that his partnership with God is not the partnership of two business men, enjoying equal rights and bargaining with one another, but rather the partnership of man and woman, or bridegroom and bride. And in this relationship he must see himself in the role of the bride and the woman. (In this school of belonging to God, by the way, the man acquires essential knowledge as to his behavior in marriage. For when he overdraws his account in being-the-man, when he, like a patriarch or pasha, turns into an unrestricted ruler and makes his wife a slave, by this form of hypertrophic pseudo-masculinity he often causes secret sufferings and utterly shattered marriages. This kind of "being-the-man," which at no time or place ever learned how to belong, does not correspond to the spirit of the New Testament. After all, Paul in 1 Cor 7:4, writes not only that the woman no longer can dispose of her body but also that the man must renounce his self-disposal for the sake of the woman. When will men ever learn this?)

Only the New Testament conceives virginity as something spiritual, something far beyond the sexual. In its light, however, the 144,000 who "were not defiled with women" (Apoc 14:4) are to be understood as neither male nor female but as those who totally belong to God. In this sense John the Baptist, whose strong masculinity nobody can deny, says in a very virginal way: "He must increase, but I must decrease" (John 3:30), and: "My joy is this — to hear the voice of the bridegroom (John 3:29). These words help us to understand the *deisis*, the central ikon of the Eastern churches' picture walls: Christ, between Mary and John the Baptist; the bridegroom between the masculine and feminine archetype. Yet both are "virgins." We can follow up this tradition in our Christian West where, on the Isenheimer Altar, Gruenewald with his *crucifixion* actually created a *deisis* of western type and, quite unhistorically, placed the archetypes of both sexes under the cross as they who receive. When Paul (Gal 2:20) says: "It is no longer I that live but Christ lives in me" he too is aiming at the same virginal basic attitude which, when applied to a man, is one of the follies of Christian faith. After Mary's "fiat," the mystery of being religious no longer consists primarily in a sky-aspiring pushiness, in masculine power and wisdom but in devotion, poverty, hunger and thirst for God who effects salvation. The woman is the more religious, not because, as is often maintained, she is more subject to feelings — which supposedly play a big role in this realm — but because by nature she is more capable of devotion and thus more easily open to God than the man is. Not *animus* but *anima* is "*naturaliter christiana*", that is, Christian by nature, says Tertullian so rightly. (Apol 17) Thus, when depth psychology (for instance C. G. Jung) already expects the man to cultivate the *anima* within himself and, for the sake of his personal perfection, to make it a part of his life-formation, how much more must the theologian address the anima also in the man, as she alone enables a chalice-like openness to God essential to Christian piety.

THREE CONCLUSIONS
1. THE JANUS-FACED POSITION OF THE PRIEST

The Priest — Representative of
Community and Vicarius Christi

It is interesting, in the light of what we have said above, to think about the position of the priest in the Church. It is actually Janus-faced. I call it this because the priest is considered to be, from one side, the representative of the community and, from the other, the representative of Christ. Since he comes from God to the community, some want him to celebrate Mass facing the community; others prefer the facelessness of the priest, as praised by Gertrud von Le Fort. The following distinction between the internal, general, and the external, special, priesthood might help to clarify this.

First of all, the priest participates in the general priesthood which is common to all the faithful through baptism.

In this sense he, like the community itself, stands before God as its exponent, and indicates with his chalice-like open hands the readiness of the community to receive God. Through him and in him is performed the marriage of the Lord with this community, his bride. From this community the priest is "selected." He represents it and thus is nameless and faceless to it. He is anonymous. This God-receiving, virginal anonymity places him in a special proximity to the Holy Spirit. He is the representation of the ones who receive.

In the realm of the general priesthood, there is a special priesthood for a special service, as Leo the Great calls it. This is the "external priesthood" which is reserved for a few.[11] This special priesthood represents the Son, the Divine bridegroom. Only the priest is allowed to say: *"Hoc est corpus meum"*, this is *my* (Christ's) body. This special priesthood, which generates into the community, is reserved for man. The *vicarius Christi* confronts the community, and, as God's instrument, conveys salvation and life. This is naturally a masculine-paternal function; yet, in order to exclude from the start every shade of false patriarchism, we should avoid the danger of equating him with God the Father.

Celibacy of the Priest

This distinction between the general and the special priesthood makes us aware of a wide-spread distortion of the image of the priest in the Church. One cannot present in the liturgy of the Mass the priest as the anonymous, God-facing, exponent of the community, so that in him and through him the "marital mystery" with the community can be performed — and, at the same time, speak of a special, Christ-representing priesthood reserved for the man. Neither can we let the priest, as coming from God, perform the liturgy facing the community — and, at the same time, extol the purely ecclesiastical law of celibacy, now history, as though it were a virginity actually demanded by the nature of the priesthood. It seems that here two images constantly shift back and forth causing confusion. If we refer to the general priesthood, then virginity, the receptive openness-to-God, is of the nature of priesthood. But if we emphasize the special, generating priesthood reserved for the man, then the coming-to-the-community must be expressed in the liturgy. In this case, celibacy remains a law of the Church and not one demanded by nature; its expediency can be discussed. There have been, as we know, centuries of fruitful priestly activity without celibacy, and Lutheran ministers converted to the Catholic Church have been allowed to remain married even after their ordination to the priesthood. The East, in the second Trullian Synod (692), made marriage compulsory for the priest. After the union with Rome, the synod of Brest-Litowsk (1596) conceded this regulation also for the future. To say it clearly once more: virginity as an expression of the betrothed community's total belongingness to God is part of the general priesthood which every Christian should live in a way that transcends the sexual, but it does not belong to the special priesthood representing Christ.

2. PRAYER IN VIRGINAL OPENNESS TO GOD

The Virgin is Prayer

Furthermore, it seems to me necessary that the virgin's disposition to listen and to be attentive be made fruitful also in the realm of prayer, which is today in a sad state and subject to general complaint. Not that I intend here to advocate a further infiltration of feminism and of certain unmanly sentimentalities. We have already changed the quotation from the Cherubian Wanderer into: every soul *must* become the bride of the Eternal Word. Hence the man, too, must strive for a form of piety which listens to and belongs to God. The man knows that prayer shoots like an arrow to get to the Father through Christ. But the woman knows that prayer can also be a listening swinging and swaying within the Holy Spirit. Worded prayer is masculine; silence and submergence is feminine. Men argue that prayer must be performed and try it. But the women sense more that one can also *be* prayer. Thus they understand the Orantes, the feminine figures in the catacomb paintings, who stand with open hands, not just praying but, more than this, themselves representing prayer. When Michelangelo, in the fresco of the Sistine Chapel, made Eve immediately after her creation fold her hands, he may have intended to represent his idea that woman is more closely related to prayer.

Silent Submergence Instead of Responsibility

"One of the most peculiar (and saddest) deceptions of modern times is the supposition that a limited series of symbols, that is, words, composed in a certain, so-called logical way, suffices to communicate not only all factual knowledge but also every kind of feeling, the intensity of every emotion and the content of every inspiration . . . Only under the pressure of tragic circumstances did we slowly begin to question the qualification of the word, and now we suspect that great areas of human experience are representable only with the help of signs and symbols; in any case, not through words, but by figure and gesture." What H. Read states here, in his report about the total "verbalization" of youth education, could be equally applied to the typically masculine total verbalization of prayer; for even in praying, man experiences today in a tragic way the limits of responsibility. Words are like coins, worn thin, without shape and without weight. They are barely good enough for superficial communication and traffic signs. To be useful for prayer, for an encounter with God, they would have to be taken back into silence, presumably for many years; only there could they once more become weighty and living, and have a generating power. Thus to suffer from one's own prayer-life can be a most healthy sign; one senses that the word-coin is of no value to God and that the use of empty shells is babble. Would not a prayer which is virginal openness to God, a listening, silent submergence in his presence and in his voice be more fruitful? After all, "silence is the true place of God" (R. Schwarz). Henri Bremond, who has inquired into the history of religious life, praises Thomassin, a great man of prayer in that "the characteristic quality of his prayers did not lie in the choice and arrangement of his words but rather in the pulsation of his soul."[12] Prayer is silence; it is to listen and to look at God with the eyes of one's heart; it is to let him speak the words of life into one's self and then, at the end, to say no more than perhaps "Amen" or "Alleluja." Only this silence of desires, actions and words — not the pause which is merely a hasty breathing-space for more and more words — leads out of the distraction into recollection and the "marital mystery" of union with God.

"Oremus"!

Under this aspect, should we not be more aware of the silence which the liturgy prescribes after the invitation "Oremus," and endure God in this silence? For this silence is the actual prayer which then is comprised in the short words of stylistically polished Roman Orations. Yet many consider it almost an annoying pause which hampers a brisk performance. Others even ignore it completely, thus waiving the grace of being surrounded and permeated by the streams of the Holy Spirit.

It would be good, too, if sometimes we would once more speak of the Mass as a sacred spectacle, as does F. Hillig.[13] During Mass, the priest says many private prayers which even the truly participating faithful do not need to say and which they should not try to find by nervously thumbing through their missals. It would be much more fruitful to spend this time in exterior and interior contemplation. In the case of a man as sensitive as Paul Claudel, this kind of participation in the Holy Mass led to his conversion. He himself writes about this: "Those were the most sublime gestures ever fitted to a human being. I could not take my eyes off the spectacle of the Mass, and every movement of the priest left a deep impression on my spirit and heart."

Prayer in Openness to God

If the piety of the man is once again to be freed from the sterility of action and responsibility, it is necessary to implant in his restless activity the shoot of a virginally receptive silence and contemplation. His clearness, austerity and sense of reality will then rehabilitate the so much maligned and misunderstood concept of piety; and the implanted shoot will lead him to a new fertility. But should he reject this shoot leaving piety only to children and women then he should neither be surprised nor complain when infantile and extremely feministic forms of piety begin to become rampant and in the end bring even healthy piety into disrepute.

3. GRACE — LOVE — BEAUTY

What is Grace?

We shall add a third excursion: How, and by what means

does God unite himself with the soul which is ready to receive? We give this streaming power which flows down and transforms nature the name grace. The classical period of eastern theology used the much stronger word "deification"; for, unmerited and unable to be forced, it makes the Christian what Christ is according to his divine nature, namely a child of the Father in heaven. In the West, however, the doctrine of grace gradually became independent and developed into a separate treatise which more and more constricted the view until it became a question of grace and freedom of will — grace and divine predestination respectively. Finally, in the eighteenth century, nothing was left of this grace but a purely moral concept. Only the 19th century again bought a turning to the essential. At this time, M. J. Scheeben, for instance, calls grace the indwelling of the Holy Spirit, thus coining an expression which has since been clarified and biblically established by G. Soehngen. Herewith theology returned to the center of the Johannine school of thought and restored a bridge to the Christian East which had become almost uncrossable. On the part of man, a spiritual attitude of virginity, a dedication open to God, is the necessary disposition for this indwelling of the Holy Spirit. In accordance with her virginal nature, the virgin is the bride of the Holy Spirit.

Love and Beauty

The indwelling of the Holy Spirit must have been something completely unknown to the pre-Christian world. They did not even have the words for it. The inspired authors of the New Testament chose the word *"charis,"* current throughout the Greek world, to designate this new state of affairs. *Charis* means charm and comeliness as well as favor and affection. Th. Haecker[14] alluded to the relationship of the Greek word *charis* with the Latin word *charitas* or *caritas* (Charity). In Latin we convey the meaning of the word for grace with *gratia*, a word which can hardly deny its proximity to the concept "beauty." For the love in which God gives himself to the soul, the indwelling of the third divine person, makes it indeed into a "beautiful soul" in the actual sense of the word. Philosophers of aesthetics have racked their brains for centuries to find an objective definition of the beautiful, and even Thomas Aquinas did not succeed when he said that the beautiful is that which, when seen, pleases. As we well know, judgment of taste varies. The beautiful would be this for one person and that for another. We could almost advocate the notion that neither philosophy nor aesthetics can totally comprehend beauty and that in the last analysis, it is a matter of theology. The indwelling of the Holy Spirit in a virginal human being, its radiance through matter, the "fragrance of immortality diffused over the surface of things" (Augustine), this is true beauty.

This *charis* cannot be forced. The *gratia* is *gratis*, that means free, unmerited and unmeritable. That is why virginity is the exact contrary of magic. Lucifer, the devil, did not want his *gratia* free. He refused to receive. Therefore he is the prime magician, because he thinks beauty can be forced.

The Beautiful God

It is especially under the aspect of virginity that we once more experience God as prime beauty. Why should only the Orthodox Church, as is their claim, preserve the thought of God's beauty radiating in the streams of the Holy Spirit? "I am the beautiful shepherd," says Jesus clearly in John's gospel (10:11) and it is characteristic that the West which at all times displays a moralizing tendency, translates *kalós* (beautiful), the word of the original text, as "good."

The beautiful shepherd's offering of his life is the prime cause of grace and hence of the beauty of the soul. The *beau Dieu* (the beautiful God), a sculpture in the Cathedral of Amiens, conveys this thought, and a song of the seventeenth century which is still sung begins with the words: "Most beautiful Lord Jesus." Thus we men of the West with our righteous way of thinking and our rationalistic approach should not leave the price of God's endowing beauty entirely up to the prayers and hymns of the East and to Dostoevski's sensitive deliberations. We confront it in virginity.

Beauty is Experienced in a Virginal Way

It would be ridiculous to believe that works of art come into existence merely by imprinting and shaping, in a very masculine way, an actively experienced form into a passively understood matter. This is the way Aristotle saw it and so it is understood by all those who think that a piece of art cannot be made without the dualism of matter and form. If this were true, art would, indeed, be connected with skillfulness. An artist would be no more than a mere artificer. But, above all, it is the artist in whom we cannot overlook the element of grace. We talk about a "gifted" artist and refer this attribute to his openness, his preparedness to receive and to make visible the beauty to which he believes himself transparent. Beauty first is always received. But only a virginal man lets himself be im-pressed by God. It is only to the degree of his communication with the Holy Spirit that man knows the beauty of the world. Only to the degree of this communication can he make it visible. When Goethe, in his song of the gardeners (*Faust II*) says: "For the temperament of woman is so closely related to art," he seems to have sensed something of this relationship of beauty to the receptive openness of the woman or, more exactly, of the virgin. This is probably the reason why the Muses always are represented as female, even though an Aristotelian interpretation of art should represent them rather as males. The virgin is the place of the presence of the Holy Spirit, and so is the work of art. For it does not reproduce what is visible, what is in the foreground, but in it becomes visible the mantle of beauty with which God has clothed matter and man. Beauty therefore resists every explanation; it wants to be experienced in a virginal way. It participates in God's inexplicable mystery. In the experience of the beautiful, all masculine longing and striving comes to rest; there it is dedicated and there it becomes happy to receive. There man, too, becomes in-spired in the word's most beautiful sense, that is, visited by the Holy Spirit.

BETRAYAL OF VIRGINITY

Vampirism: A Distortion

Many a woman's interior and exterior manifestation stands out boldly from the background of our hitherto existing reflections. Is not the God-open spirituality of the woman, manifested most purely by the virgin, betrayed, suspected and derided a million times? Instead of the devotion which should be woman's most prominent characteristic, a misinterpreted notion of equality and imitated masculinity has produced the *vamp*. A "one-sex-doctrine" has created this type which is the exact contrary to the virgin: every relatedness to the other pole is egotistically denied. Just as masculine monogenism leads to sadism (cf. Weininger: "coitus is related to murder"), feminine unipolarity leads to vampirism. Thus, like those terrible spiders who are known to devour their males, the vamp, too, wants to "consume" everything in her environment, and especially the man. Instead of the devotion which is natural to the woman, she demands pleasure and by means of pleasure destroys through diabolical cunning. But with this, the world becomes more and more empty for mankind. Everything is pulled into the great undertow, is destroyed by consuming, and the psychological reaction to the resulting air of coldness is a boredom already described by Pascal (the psychic counterpart of the vacuum likewise demonstrated by Pascal). For only the virgin who patiently and preparedly waits and expects that things, men and God will be what they really are allows everything to maintain its own self and individual worth.

The Man's Fear

In principle, every human being can become a vamp. For the woman, however, it represents a most serious perversion of her nature. Also, we should not think that vampirism is a modern invention — an invention let's say, of those who talk about "love" as an activity of success and who "practice" it in this sense. Where else could originate man's age-old love of infatuating sirens, of nymphs and pixies, of undines, dryads and Circes who entice in order to destroy? It seems, though, that in our times vampirism is especially widespread, highly paid and proudly talked about.

When men talk about women in military terms that is, when they "besiege," "storm," "capture," "use" women, this way of speaking and its corresponding behavior shows a lack of sensitivity, tact and nobleness of mind, but it still lies within a somewhat stretched idea of masculinity. But when the woman makes the man her prey, this is not a stretched femininity but rather a result of perversion, of a complete distortion of everything feminine. What ought to be waiting openness, becomes a magic force. And nothing is more contrary to feminine nature than such magic. The attracting power of the sexes, intended by God, is abused and unilaterally misused.

The Pin-Up-Girl, an Artificial "Beauty"

Another, equally unpleasant and wide-spread distortion of feminine nature is the pin-up-girl. She is expected to bring her made-up "beauty" to market as a model for advertising or as a stimulant in masculine circles. The pin-up-girl and, even more, her managers, expect hard cash for publicizing and exploiting her bodily measurements. On the one hand, the exhibition-business in such "sex-dolls" has already pushed the man's erotic stimulus-threshold to the point that nothing but the strongest aphrodisiacs in word and picture can make him feel attracted by the woman. On the other hand, a true meeting between man and woman suffers from this standardized piece-work, since it blocks out, in the depths of man's soul, the vital factors evoking erotic attraction. For often a true woman cannot win the contest with the mask-like idol.

The Mendacious Canon of Pagan Beauty

We said of the virgin, the purest representation of womanhood, that God becomes present in her dedication. In her openness and expectation, she is the place of the presence of the Holy Spirit who alone gives true and living beauty. Instead of this attitude and devotion, the cult of modern "beauty queens" pursues workmanship — the "put-on-job". Masseurs, face-specialists, plastic surgeons and other so-called "beauticians" try to "correct" God's "imperfect" creation and to produce a new "beauty" synthetically. "We are united by what is beautiful," says Claudel (*Satin Slipper*) and with this he reminds us of the power of the personal bond in the Holy Spirit. The artificial and standardized beauty is a parody of this effect of the union in the Holy Spirit. In thousands of American "charm schools" an almost world-standardized mask is being "created." Behind all the chemical formulas and anti-wrinkle creams necessary to produce it is the profane demand to create an artificial counter-nature antagonistic to all individuality. It is logical that this body, which is no longer accepted, is not allowed to age. The pagan falsehood of the possibility of eternal youth on earth is once more propagated and the flinty and totally unveiled faces close their mind to knowledge about aging, and the mellow, peaceful and lucid beauty proper to it.

MARY, *vas spirituale*

In Mary, The World Says "Fiat"

Mary is the beginning and re-beginning of woman since she is, first and above all, virgin. She is the spirit-ual virgin, *vas spirituale*, the spiritual vessel belonging to the Holy Spirit. Her first word, handed down to us in the bible, is still the cautious question springing from an Old Testament way of thinking: "How shall this happen since I do not know man?" (Luke 1:34) But when God's messenger goes on: "The Holy Spirit shall come upon thee and the power of the Most High shall overshadow thee," she answers with that virginal, receptive *"fiat,"* that is, let it be done. We already mentioned above, that with the New Testament begins the hour of the moved. No more words of priests and prophets. They did not draw salvation down to earth. Only the response of the Virgin who is "blessed because she has believed" (Luke 1:45) rendered to mankind the great service of salvation.

In Jesus Christ, God's word became flesh. Mary spoke her personal yes and, beyond this, the yes of all mankind. With this *"fiat"* she did not merely render a functional service; in her virginal being-the-response she represents the deepest nostalgia and the highest possibility of all creation. When the angel calls Mary "full of grace," the angel's and the Church's praise mean the same. The grace, of which Mary is full, is God's beauty which streamed into her through the overshadowing of the Holy Spirit. Every virginal soul totally resting in God will be agleam in this glory.

"Beautiful Like The Moon . . ."

The praying Church celebrates the Virgin Mary with the words that she is "beautiful like the moon and terrible like an army in array." A deep truth is hidden in this phrase. The moon does not shine by itself. It reflects the light it receives from the sun. It is not splendor but reflection. Among the many virtues we can find in Mary, this is the highest: to be receptive and devoted. But this virtue is not so much a matter of morals but rather one of being, so that it is actually the "dedicating power of the cosmos" (Gertrud von Le Fort) — made flesh. As Nikolaus von Lenau writes in his poem "Savonarola," Mary, who received, represents the total nostalgia of mankind. We may cite Paul's word: "the weak things of the world has God chosen to put to shame the strong" (1 Cor 1:27). At all times, this has been a stumbling block of Christendom which the man feels inclined to believe untrue. Yet also he must learn to be beautiful like the moon; for it is not masculine power which forces God to come down but a receptive virginity in which he can give himself.

". . . Terrible Like An Army in Array"

The Church also calls the Virgin "terrible like an army in array." Is such a word not repulsive? Does it not strike us as strange since we are used to seeing in the Virgin only what is lovable and attractive? But, as we already know, the Virgin is at the same time a martyr. She is not only the place of God's presence in the world but also a citadel. Therefore we praise Mary in the litany — the invocations of which could, in a mysterious way, be applied also to the Holy Spirit — as the "tower of ivory." In the midst of men, taken up only with themselves, with their innerworldly goals and concerns, the Virgin defends the bastion of God. God alone has access to her, and only when he enters does her soul begin to sing. But for everything noisy and obtrusive the Virgin is an "army in array." Her beauty is valiant. In a soul which wants to be totally occupied by God there is no place for the much-too-much which, while often being petty, wants to be taken seriously. The Virgin is not a compromise with the world, she is definitiveness. She does not like the as-well-as, but the either-or. The Virgin is a sword.

Come, Lord!

Just as the Virgin is at the beginning of our salvation so is she also at the end of it. When the great advent of mankind finally approaches the goal of its pilgrimage there will stand once more "the bride adorned for her husband" (Apoc 21:2). The Spirit, as it says in the Apocalypse, will be the leader of the bride and the bride will say the word of the mystery of marital union: "Come!" "And let him who hears say: 'Come!'" (Apoc 22:17). Then (Apoc 21:6) he who is the Alpha and the Omega will, to him who thirsts, give freely of the fountain of the water of life. Then there will be the eternal wedding feast, the mysterious union of God and the Virgin.

Chapter 3

THE HOLY SPIRIT AND THE WOMAN ARE GOD'S GREAT "AND"

THE POWER OF SOCIALIZATION

Father-and-Son

Our God is three persons and triune at the same time. In our introductory remarks (page 5) we already pointed out that Christian monotheism is different from Islamism and Judaism. At the same time, however, we must avoid applying the picture of the human family, that is father, mother and child, to the trinity of God. Augustine already emphasizes that the adoption of this image makes it difficult to avoid the danger of a three-God-doctrine. Our wondering and worshiping meditation best starts with the thought: *"God exists in the way of love."* But love asks for unity and plurality, for identity and difference, for richness of being and ability to give and receive, for fullness within oneself and the going out of oneself . . . "God is love" (1 John 3:8). True love demands a plurality of persons. The desire of love wants to eliminate the distance between the lover and the beloved without destroying their difference. This remains a dream on earth; therefore human love is restless. This going beyond the loving beloved and the beloved lover, which creatures hunt for in vain, within God is one single person. The Holy Spirit is love itself; not the act of love. The act of love is the divine nature — but the Holy

Spirit is the living bond, the interpersonal relationship of the persons with one another who dwell in the love. As the Father's love for the Son and the Son's love for the Father, the Holy Spirit is brought forth by both, without bringing forth anything himself . . . "The peculiarity of the Holy Spirit consists in being what each person has in common with the other" (Augustine). Thus God exists in the way of love; he is the prime image of every fellowship. The Holy Spirit is subsistent love, as theologians express it, and Paul already in his time attributes fellowship to him (2 Cor 13:13). This is not a mere phrase; it means that, while the quality of giving oneself applies to all three persons, it corresponds in a mysterious way especially to the personality of the Holy Spirit and to his position in the eternal streaming forth. He, who does not pass on the divine life to a fourth person, is the one from whom comes the communion within the Trinity. "In God, the name love can be taken in a natural as well as in a personal way. And in so far as it is taken personally, it is the name proper to the Holy Spirit, just as *word* is the name proper to the Son" (S.theol.I, 37:1). The Holy Spirit is the fusion of the Father and Son, the mutual breathing of love. Therefore theologians call him also the "kiss" of the Father and the Son, or *vinculum*, the divine, personal bond. Thinking of the entire Trinity, we could certainly also say "Father And Son" and with this we would have called all three persons by the names proper to their nature. Yet this "And" is not an additive "And," but the personal copula uniting the Father and the Son. The Holy Spirit is, we could say, the *catholic* personality within the threefold God, since in his personal love he unites the three persons into one.

Supernature — And — Nature

The Holy Spirit continues the mystery of his eternal

origin in his temporal mission in so far as he, with the streams of his grace brings the world and mankind home to God. Through him and with him it is no longer: "God here, and the world there," but "God *and* the world"; no longer "God on the one hand and man on the other," but "God *and* man." Karl Barth once called this idea the fundamental heresy of Catholicism and, in fact, it is simply the catholic idea. In the Holy Spirit, God's catholic "And," God and man remain united with one another. This cannot even be changed by sin, the actual nature of which consists in refusing or in culpably neglecting the ever-existent possibility of God's communion with man. In the Holy Spirit, God's love urges to communion.

Therefore it can very easily happen that what we harmlessly call "secularization" is not some kind of sin but sin itself. The secularization of life, which extricates more and more areas from their original relatedness to God, this at times violent and at other times inattentive separation, with the secret or open purpose of completely untying God from the world, is diametrically opposed to the wooing of God who in the Holy Spirit zealously seeks out man's love. The freedom argued for by art and science is not necessarily the freedom of the Holy Spirit; the joy in secular feasts and celebrations is not always the joy which is fruit of the spirit of joy. This universal secularizing process often finds its apex in the proclamation of a purely secular, entirely worldly paradise. But when not only the fanatic masses of bolshevism but also natural scientists of the western mentality believe in this utopia; when they consider the advent-like expectation of the new Jerusalem — coming down out of heaven, the gates of which are pearls and the street of which is pure gold, as it were transparent glass (Apoc 21:21) — to be but miserable promises for weaklings, they are unaware of the fact that this weakness is of virginal nature. It is breathing and living within the Holy Spirit.

The Holy Spirit, The Embracing Power

And in a third sense the Holy Spirit is the great "And." He not only unites Father and Son into a Triunity and embraces supernature and nature, he embraces in his catholicity all great tensions and schisms in the world. He makes the tensions fruitful and tries to heal the schisms. With his descending at the first Pentecost, he dispels the Babel of tongues through the "baptism of the native langauge of the people." All those who through him are in a state of sober drunkenness can understand one another, since he allows them to speak in their mother tongue (Apoc 2:8). But man's mother tongue is the language of the Holy Spirit, the spirit of fellowship and of love. "Unite us all into a community of the one holy pneuma" the Basilian liturgy still prays in the solemn invocation of the spirit. We live in the "covenant of the spirit" (2 Cor 3:6).

The less men are united in spirit, the more the wall of not understanding grows around them. Although they may use the same phonetics and syntax, understanding will become more and more difficult. The "walls" we see erected everywhere in the world (Jerusalem, Berlin) are visible expressions of the inner spirit-lessness which starts with this lack of understanding and which ends in a general chaos. God does not want mankind in separated army camps, no matter whether they are under religious banners or political emblems. These kinds of separation are sinful, too. Thus the Holy Spirit is rightly invoked for the gift of language in which the mother tongue is again spoken and understood. And in the hymn of Pentecost we ask him: "Bend the stubborn" (rigid attitudes, intolerant kinds of spirit-lessness), "Melt the frozen" (frozen in problems, hearts turned into stones), "On our dryness pour thy dew" (humorlessness, hopeless confusion). When Pope John XXIII, abandoning the hitherto used vocabulary, talked about a "reconciliation" with our brothers, instead of "subjection"

or "return," we can call this a spirit-ual diction. For —
as already mentioned — in the Holy Spirit, sinners and
saints are united with one another, and God gives his grace
also to those outside of the Church (a fact which Clement
XI, in his bull *"Unigenitus,"* so fiercely defended against
the Jansenists). The dialectic pincers-attack on the truth
might be a first step in finding it, but a deeper insight will
be gained through a spirit-ual paradox which involves also
the golden granule of the "heretic".

Thus the Holy Spirit is an enemy of every separation. He
unites, gathers and makes tensions fruitful so that in them
the higher and the permanent value might be found. Spirit
and flesh, old *and* young, man *and* woman, East *and* West,
white *and* colored, poor *and* rich, eros *and* agape — this
is what is intended by the "kiss" of the Father and the Son,
the divine bond, the spirit of union and fellowship: the
great, catholic, three times "And" of God.

God's Image in the Union of Love

In an analogous manner we can apply the aforementioned thought also to man: Man, too, "exists in the way of
love." In Genesis we read: "It is not good that man be
alone" (2:18). Thinking out the meaning of this word, we
can conclude that the man is not man in the fullest sense
of the word. He needs an "equal" whom he knows and by
whom he is known, needs the "help at his side." Through
woman it becomes evident that man exists but as one who
loves, that he is himself only when comprehending himself
as oriented towards the other. Man as God's image can be
fully represented only in the union of love. It is only in his
relationship to the other, in his relationship of love, that
he puts his trinitarian character into practice.

We may perhaps also risk the statement that already in
the creation of man as "man and woman", the archetype of
the mystical body has been modeled. Paul's words: "This is

a great mystery — I mean in reference to Christ and to the Church" (Eph 5:32) doubtlessly can be explained also in this sense.

The Coming Forth of Eve

Let us add another train of thought. It originated in gnosticism and we are far from granting it the rank of a proof. But it may serve as a picture, as an eidetic image, to show us the forms and the intensity with which human spirit tried to explain the inevitable and essential fact of the togetherness of man and woman.

Eve comes forth from the *"sela"* (the Hebrew word) of Adam. *"Sela"* is the rib so frequently referred to in mythical thinking; the insecurity of the translators, alone, should advise more caution. *"Sela"* means "vault," "pregnant part," or "weight-carrying side." Eve was, in a mysterious way, already within Adam. In any case, Genesis wants to talk about a kind of "delivery" by Adam from his pregnant side.

But what kind of sleep was this *"tardemah"* of Adam? Following our lead, the state of sleep into which Adam falls is the figurative expression for God's presence. He becomes world-aspiring. World-aspiration is the sleep of the foolish virgins in the Lord's parable. To rise from the sleep of world-aspiration is Paul's exhortation to the Romans (13:11) and the Church's admonition to the advent-minded Christians. Originally Adam was completely devoted to God, undivided, virginal. His sleep is perhaps the remembrance of a sin before the sin. An arising tendency towards the world begins to separate Adam from God, and the marriage of the virginal Adam with his Lord is in jeopardy. In order to stop the vertical fall, God delivers the hitherto undivided Adam into the divided-into-two masculine and feminine human being. He delivers him physically and spiritually. "Adam lost the virgin and received the woman" says Jacob Boehme. Up to then, he was attracted by virginity, now the existence of the woman at least saves him from fall and absolute separation. Man becomes marital. "But the married man is divided" (1 Cor 7:33). While the relation of the virgin points to the vertical, marital man looks to the horizontal. Coming from one flesh, man and woman strive to again become one flesh. "She, now," (Gen 2:23) says Adam almost relieved. From now on life is a synthesis. The need of this synthesis is, even now, time and again regally overcome by the virgin, but the self-complacency of Narcissus denies it in a false "autarchy." Therefore the virgin remains fertile in the original sense while Narcissus must be sterile.

The Help at His Side

In former times educational principles of society provided only two forms of womanhood for a girl. Either she remained unmarried — and then it was completely up to her to give this kind of life a higher meaning or more or less adjust herself — or else she married and soon was completely absorbed in her maternal obligations. The time of love, the period of engagement, during which she was interested exclusively in the man, was short and left only fleeting memories in her future married life. Only two relationships were conceivable for woman: as virgin the relationship to God; as woman the motherly relationship to children. Thus whole centuries failed to recognize that in marriage the women is first the companion of the man. She is "helper, assistant, is like himself" (Gen 2:20). Who, by the way, when hearing the word "helper," does not immediately think of the Holy Spirit whom the Lord himself called "advocate" (John 16:7)? So, the second symbol by which we represent figuratively the nature of woman is the symbol of semi-circles coordinated to one another. Without one another, man and woman would be defective and helpless.

A Promise, Never Completely Fulfilled

However, we would only mystify marriage and its possibilities should we overlook the residue of unfulfillment which, regardless of the form and degree of union, still remains. No matter how ardent the desire of love might be, a creature is never able to establish that kind of unity which lives in the divine original of the Trinity. Claudel once called woman a "promise which is never completely fulfilled." Therefore marriage is not only a gift but always a task too. Its most important service consists in allowing two human beings to sense their human imperfectness, to experience the holy reminder which will be truly fulfilled only in eternal life. "The goal of every love is that two become one," says the Russian philosopher of religion, Florensky. In their community at the table the spouses try, with the poverty of the word, to declare their love, and to absorb the intruding outside into this love-conversation. But since there is no fulfillment, they believe that they will find peace in the highest form of mutual "knowing," in the exciting becoming-one-flesh. Yet also here they soon must find out that their nostalgia was greater than what was attained. We tend to interpret the comment that every being is sad after the coitus in merely physiological terms; or else we try to interpret it as a confirmation for a devaluation of the sexual in a Christian guise. But might it not be that in this very comment is the secret awareness of the sadness experienced by man when marital knowing does not fulfill what it promised?

Fulfillment in the Eternal Wedding Feast

Even the eucharistic community at the table, where the

spouses are united with one another in the Lord (to my mind, by the way, the main reason against so-called mixed marriage, which cannot realize the eucharistic *communio* in the Lord), is merely the "pledge of the future glory." Only a participation in the eternal wedding feast, where the lamb of God will be the imperishable nourishment of the resurrected, gives that kind of union which all forms of expression of love promise, prophesy, and yet are not able to fulfill.

Our Lord, asked when the kingdom of God will come, answered, in a nonscriptural account (Agraphon, second letter to Clement): "When two will become one and the outer like the inner and man one with woman, when there is neither masculine nor feminine." These words are very akin to Matthew's statement (22:30): "For at the resurrection they will neither marry nor be given in marriage, but will be as angels of God in heaven." Antagonism to marriage has often misinterpreted this in the sense of complete sexlessness. But it rather seems to be understood in the sense that sexual differences will be taken out of their temporary state and harbored in a final union. "It has not yet appeared what we shall be," (1 John 3:2) but the loving longing for one another here on earth is a promising shadow of the happiness there. What is promised to the polarity of the sexes in intercourse will find its happy fulfillment in the "eternal rest." Thus the almost theological meaning of the song,

> "Man and wife and wife and man
> follow their creator's plan"

reveals itself.

EROS AND *AGAPE*, *THIS* AND *THAT* KIND OF LOVE

Love Unites

We have seen that love is that power in which man and

woman are drawn to one another, the power of uniting here, which points to a perfect union there. However, the concept of love is extremely ambiguous. It not only reflects the biological development and a long history of man; this ambiguity is also the result of the diversity of objects which love can choose and of the multiplicity of relations in which love acts. Generally speaking we can say that mankind did not lose the presentiment that things and men should be united in love in spite of the debris left by Adam's sin (separation). Love is therefore a holy and utterly defensible remnant of a paradise never completely lost. Man feels more or less clearly that all things and all men are intended for one another, and senses it as comforting when, through love, he can reunite a few fragments once more. Unconsciously he longs for this future union in which the lion and the lamb again play with one another.

Different Forms of the One Love

Besides the forms of love, known as empathy and friendship, helpfulness and sympathy, there are, precisely, three forms which define the relationship between man and woman: sexual attraction, erotic love, and "heavenly" love. The two last-named are also called *eros* and *agape*.

The *sexual* attraction of one human being for another already contains elements of choice. Consequently it differs from the instinct of the animal, even though well-meaning educators may maintain the contrary. But the choice is directed primarily to bodily qualities of the partner, which are temporary. Therefore a relationship based solely on sexual attraction easily changes partners. Very unjustly, *erotic love* is equated with sexual attraction. Yet this kind of love already experiences in the physical presence of the beloved a happiness of soul and spirit, which the lover makes every effort to keep. With jewelry and clothes, with

happy frolicsomeness and kisses, flirting, playing and danc-
ing, it looks for ever new means to express this desire.
Therefore, according to times and cultures erotic love can
manifest itself in very different forms. The pastoral roman-
ces of the eighteenth century are quite different from the
erotic literature of ancient or medieval love-poetry. Even
in situations where the material means everything and the
spiritual little or nothing, or, to go even further, where
eros is deliberately suppressed for the sake of the biologico-
political interest as in parts of Russia and China, *eros*
knows how to maintain its claim.

The source of *agape* is God. Originating in him, it floods
into the heart of man who strives to become more and more
transparent and to pass on God's love, through himself, to
the beloved fellowman. The physical aspect of the others
therefore plays only a secondary role. Even a bodily dis-
figurement can be lovable, since it is reflecting the countenance of the suffering Lord. What is essential is that both
lover and beloved be bearers of personal values and striving to carefully cultivate these values.

What Does "True Love" Mean?

The problem in which we are interested here is the confusion which is caused, on the one hand, by a lack of sufficient differentiation among these three forms of love and,
on the other hand, by the — erroneous — opinion that it
is a matter of hierarchical values. In reality, these are
simply three possibilities of a loving meeting, which must
not exclude one another, and can exist side by side. The
much used notion, "true" love, which only admits agape,
which disapproves of sexual attraction and does away with
eros as something insincere, unnecessary and frivolous,
must be considered a great danger. Only when the person
engaging in sexual experience is immature, or when his

guiding image contains pseudo-sexual substitutes so that the partner is actually used as a means of self-satisfaction — in other words, when one form of love is isolated from the other — can we no longer speak about true love. But this danger exists in any one of the three forms of love, and not only in the area of the sexual and erotic.

The "Lower and the Higher" Forms of Love

A. Nygren,[15] a Swedish Lutheran bishop, wrote a very thorough work on eros and agape which unfortunately has confused rather than clarified the meaning of the concept of love. This study created the general impression that it is a matter of two different kinds of love, which exclude one another. Catholic groups, too, have taken up his idea. The New Testament, however, knows only one kind of love, and the German and English languages with only the one word (*Liebe*, love) for all its forms, are very akin to the spirit of scripture. But, together with Holy Scripture, we have to distinguish very clearly between the different motives of love. Man cannot put agape side by side or in the place of sexual or erotic love. Rather agape should embrace and permeate all areas of life, preserving their independence and value. In the sexual encounter two become so much "one flesh" that now in agape the other is loved "as his own flesh." Whoever, in the sexual meeting, thinks only of himself, whoever in erotic love hopes merely to find himself again, isolates himself from his partner, and sins, because his sexus and eros are not embraced by agape.

Eros and Agape Seek One Another

From this we can see that the love in which man and woman must become united to one another must dispense with the separation of eros and agape, and that a purely spiritual concept of love and the constant talk about the necessity of sublimation — that is, the conversion of the "inferior" form of love into the "superior" — leads to the neglect of physical expressions of love and to shyness toward eros and sexus. As a result, one does not take the sexual otherness of his partner seriously and even believes that with these tempered marital relations he practices a higher form of Christianity. But while it is true that, wherever love has cooled, not even the most skillful erotic technique can cure a marriage, it is just as true that the disregard of the physical in one's partner, masked in pious words, can indicate a lack of love with grave consequences. Daily erotic pleasantness and tenderness are indispensable for the happiness of a marriage.

Origen simply equated platonic eros with Christian agape. According to our deliberations, this is and remains false. Yet they do not differ so much that one would have to choose: either eros or agape. We must distinguish between them but not separate them. Otherwise it could happen that agape is placed so far above human reality that the so-called wordly love, eros, turns into a forbidden lust. We can easily refer to numerous examples in history to show this. We should not say eros *or* agape but rather eros *and* agape. Here again we have the catholic "And."

Soloviev went deeper into our problem than did Origen. He questions why Plato used the word eros for love since he could just as well have chosen other words like philia or agape. He thinks that the reason for this is that eros comprises both the sensual urge and an ascent into the infinite-eternal. Therefore, when Plato calls it a task of eros to "procreate in beauty," he meant to express his idea that eros should be able to go beyond the animalistic and not at all beautiful act of procreation and allow man to experience a kind of transfiguration. He believes that the thought of the needed salvation of man's corporality was the primary reason why Plato used the word eros; for in eros itself lies the vague urge for immortality which, within man, reaches its apex in a longing to enter the eternal. A theory indeed worth thinking about, the practice of which Christendom occasionally overlooked but has never completely forgotten.

Neither should we make the mistake of considering the distance between eros and sexus, which, because of the general nadir of morals, Christendom in the fourth century was obliged to effect, as actual Christian doctrine. The propagation of an ascesis antagonistic to eros, which is the price of a merely negatively understood chastity, and a virginity hostile to sex, which hardly can hide its gnostic origin, contradicts a healthy doctrine which accepts God's entire creation.

Thomas says that, before paradise was lost, marriage was better than perfect chastity. Thus in his opinion man's sexuality is not contradictory to a supernature achieved through grace. This conception, which we also find in Dante and later on in Petrarch, is not, as Berdyaev says, a "lame compromise with the fallen world" but a sign of the finally regained order. We know that even after the fall of man progression in grace does not demand the abstention from eros but merely its subjection to a permeating agape. For "eros and agape seek one another." (K. Pfleger) This seeking one another is the affirmation of the power of the world which God sends forth out of himself so that they may again return to him. The Middle Ages had no "sexual problem" or "sexual instruction" and its pertinent literature. They did not know prudishness nor the characteristic narrowing-down of the concept of morality which came only with Calvin and which brought about the disastrous entry of Puritanism into the continent. A. Adam[16] traced its consequences even on our everyday language.

The Two-In-One Flame

Only in the twentieth century has eros again been re-habilitated and, characteristically, first in the Catholic world. Claudel, for instance, although his first love was sinful, never belittled the power and the meaning of eros. Already before him, Leon Bloy emphasized the "and" between eros and agape in beautiful language. To the bride who wrote her stormy wooer that she certainly loved God more than him he answered: "Dear child, what do you know about this? I, for my part, could not write something like that to you. And I could not do it for I am not able to undertake such a division. I love God in you, through you, because of you. I love you perfectly in God as a Christian shall love his wife. The idea to tear asunder this two-in-one flame of love is for me sophistry, is a notion which does not even enter my mind."[17] Such thoughts are strikingly but-tressed by the philosopher Gabriel Marcel.[18] According to him, to exist never means merely *"sum"* (I am), but *"sur-sum"* (I am lifted beyond myself). Christian personality is created only by surpassing itself on the whole scale of be-ing. It becomes mature only when it goes constantly towards the thou. Eros is one of the God-given possibilities to effect this *sursum*; it is the high springboard where man can push off to swing out into agape. Eros is the natural urge to find true love in the polarity of sexual tension, but not to find sex in the love. Thus eros expands into a "principle of hope" which, as we know, is something specifically Chris-tian. We may even say perhaps that eros and agape stand to one another like nature to grace. Some Protestant theo-logians, Karl Barth for instance, may consider this the fun-damental sin of Catholicism; they may see in sin a gap which only God can bridge and man is unable to make the least contribution. Yet we believe that it is only the catholic "and" of this "two-in-one flame" which saves man on the one hand from a pseudo-spiritualism and, on the other, from an autonomous sexual materialism.

The Tragic Separation

"*Fugit amor,*" love is gone: Rodin gave this name to a sculpture which represents a man and a woman standing on an unhewed, chaos-like stone, wanting to put their arms around one another, but who, because of a certain inner force, can no longer embrace. With this the sculptor meant to portray our time in which eros is vanishing. True, the machinelike character of modern man, his pragmatic thinking, the overcultivated striving for power, in the process of which love has been reduced to technique, trick and skill, are decisive factors of this inability to love. These are, by the way, all typically masculine causes which make the relationship of the sexes degenerate into a primitive kind of satisfaction of one's needs and into a cold war. But another cause, which should not be underrated, can certainly be found in the fact that, because of a completely uncatholic separation, eros has been degraded into a forbidden lust which, following the law of isolation, has degenerated into neurosis. Every year, thousands of sexologists publish books from the medical, the psychotherapeutic or the so-called marriage-counselor's viewpoint, which promise the greatest possible happiness. Yet those counseled, to their regret, must experience time and again that techniques do not yet convey happiness. Only a well-founded doctrine which is at once eros *and* agape, amor *and* caritas — a union which disempowers the taboos, the false prudery and the numerous prejudices — can produce this happiness. But where are the Christian "erologists" who, standing on the sound foundation of dogma, teach this kind of love with a good conscience and without being molested?

Here lies, in fact, one of the main concerns in our endeavor for man. For as eros in man signifies a sort of unifying center, it can be the source of infinite happiness as well as the cause of manifold disturbances. God alone knows how many frigidities, how many broken marriages and unnerved persons, how many legal rapes, how many cases of infertility are caused by a false education hostile to eros. There are still far too many who, because of false taboos, are hindered from penetrating into a love in which eros is sheltered and protected by agape. In their marriage, they know only the sexual which they believe to be a means for the higher purpose of procreating children, or else only a purely spiritual agape. Since they have never heard a theological word about eros but, on the contrary, have experienced it merely as an insincere means of propaganda or in the context of questionable amusement, they consider eros as less valuable, perhaps even as sinful in itself.

The Banishment of Eros

Former prisoners of war and modern tourists through Russia speak occasionally, with a "moralistically" raised finger, about the "cleanness" that is evident there. The dances and manners of youth, the means of advertising, the form and content of movies, are very much de-eroticized. And everywhere freshness and clearness predominate; the harassing fire of eros is stopped. While, of course, we are far from rejecting this "cleanness" or even more from believing that any western swampflower is more appropriate for youth, we need to call to mind the ideological sources which led to the banishment of eros from the Soviet's life. These sources are in no case of religious or moral nature in the Christian sense of the word. Their patron is Hegel, just as he is in regard to dialectic materialism in general. In his work *Phenomenology of the Spirit*, he writes relative to our subject: "In the house of morality, it is not *this* man, not *this* child, but *a* man, children in general; not sensitivity, but generality, on which woman's relationships rests." In simpler and clearer words this means that for the woman the man has no face. She has to carry out her womanly functions in their generality. Communism could merely affirm this thought. For nothing so much interferes with the fulfillment of the established goals and with the incorporation of man into a civilization of termites as the human face. This is also the reason that they consistently banish eros from their social order since it is the very thing which stirs up the revolt of the personal and private against the general and the collective. The vital spontaneity of eros which, we know, is a basic power of life itself, the oscillation back and forth between and I and the Thou, are beyond the control of the apparatus of the state. But only what can be controlled counts, and receives the title of virtue. Eros is always oscillating between an I and a Thou, thus being a natural enemy of the impersonal "one." Eros wants to hold on and to preserve; but the impersonal "one" wants to "travel light."

Part of "traveling light" and necessary for a better functioning society, according to bolshevism, seems to be masculinization of woman. Here it does not matter whether the masculinization of woman led to the banishing of eros or the banished eros to her masculinization. But it is certain that this causes the relationship of the sexes to be largely reduced to a comradeship of workers, and to an occasional incumbent and joyless procreating of children; for, along with the erotic, everything personal, sensitive, tender and charming is also banished from the relationship between the sexes. De-eroticized, they miss certain forms of play, which constitute important elements of freedom and of the spirit. If Huizinga's theory is right that play is one of the roots of culture, we may conclude that what is missing in this unplayful, almost "brutishly serious" comradeship of workers and community of the sexes is precisely culture. As is well-known, reason and hygiene alone cannot solve the problem of man and woman belonging to one another. They lead to a perversion of love which hypocritically and mendaciously uses this name, and finally to the state where the two sexes differ from one another only biologically by their undeniable sexual characteristics: male and female. Then the old Hindu saying becomes true: "Wherever Shakti (that is, the woman's power to delight) dies, men, in the end, dry up, too."

Eros Subjugated to Nature's Purpose

But let us come back to our world. We do not want to throw stones when we ourselves live in glass houses. Many a word spoken from the pulpit, in instructions and in the confessional are a far cry from Pius XII's address to the newly married (October 23, 1940), in which he speaks about "sensual love and its healthy joys, with its natural affection and its enthusiasm, with its spiritual union and its pleasures." Have we not failed, far too long, to recognize the personal value of the union of bodies, granting ethical value solely to the pursuit of nature's purpose? In our marriage instructions, have we not considered as the essential only the procreation of children while seldom presenting and even more seldom answering the question of the highest goal of mutual love? Yet, according to Dietrich von Hildebrand, the goal of the marriage act is procreation, but — and this is decisive — not in the sense of an instrumental function but according to the "principle of overflowing fullness." Only in the animal is the sexual urge the means of the preservation of the species. But the meaning of the union

of two human beings is the union itself. To its unique fulfillment — and in an overflowing fullness — is simultaneously entrusted the good of the offspring. More clearly
formulated this means: In the case of an instrumental link-
age (and apparently theologians have understood and explained the finality of the marital act in this sense), the
meaning and value of that which serves as a means is completely dependent on the goal to which it leads, while the
good which serves the purpose of overflowing fullness has
its meaning of existence first in itself. "Thus," says Hildebrand, "some maintain that God has put love into the hearts
of man and woman, the longing for marital union, as a
mere means for the procreation of children. But this is a
failure to understand the true character of the relationship
between marriage and the procreation of children."[19] It
would indeed be hardly compatible with the dignity of the
person, if his deepest experiences would be considered to
be a mere means which in God's eyes is to serve an ex-
trinsic purpose.

The Necessity to Eliminate Taboos

It is not the theologian's task to teach the personal
formation, education and cultivation of eros. But he is
called upon and obliged to give them foundation and
motivation so that the problem may be solved positively,
not negatively. And it is certainly not positive when in the
theology of sex "the sins are hanging around like sausages
in a meat market" (I. Lepp) and the Christian is constantly urged to ignore or to steer clear of certain tabooed areas
of life like a slalom skier weaving through the posted flags.
Agape wants to permeate all areas of life, wants to form
and to order them. For very easily a failure in the formation
of such central areas of life leads to meaninglessness and
sterility in other areas, even the spiritual. The saying "love
is blind," is valid only in a very limited area of the affective

life. Basically, love makes one see. It is neither cross-eyed nor afraid of taboos. We cannot agree with Freud and his disciples when they consider taboos antagonistic to love as the essence of Christian morals. Therefore the goal of our educational efforts must be the increase rather than the improverishment of affectivity. One who from the start excludes entire areas of life from his self-formation must give to every clear-headed person the impression of being insecure, immature and weak. The sphere of eros, too, is subject to Paul's command: "Glorify God and bear him in your body" (1 Cor 6:20).

THE NECESSARY FORMATION OF EROS

Further Progress Can Become A Throw-back

At this point it may be permitted to buttress our explanations with the insights of depth psychology. Inspired by H. Marcuse's[20] very original observations, we shall question that basic thesis of Freud according to which culture and civilization can exist only at the cost of a constant repression of the drives and, particularly, of eros. In Freud's opinion, the pleasure-principle and the reality-principle are irreconcilable. Only the constant use of reason as well as firm law and order are able to modify the pleasure drive to the degree of becoming acceptable in society. Is this not also — if we may formulate the cautious question — often the "Christian" argumentation? Is the generally much reviled Freud here not in touch with many a preacher? H. Marcuse asks rightly whether atomic bombs, concentration camps and police terror are actually — as is said offhandedly — "a throw-back into barbarianism," or whether they do not rather lie in the exaggerated concept of a total subjection of nature to the "intellectual animal." Modern intellect, autocratic and unrelated to nature, is inflated by the pride of its own proficiency and yet its perfect abominations are consequences more serious than many a barbarism. Is it not the intellect which also tears life into many little pieces and atomizes it, while eros strives to unite what is separated and thus becomes a life-preserving power?

Primacy of the Purpose of Procreation?

In order to meet ever more adequately the demands of world-transforming work and social organization, man's body, originally completely erogenous (responsive to erotic pleasure) has become progressively de-eroticised. Entire physical areas, among them also the proximity senses (taste, smell) became tabooed. Social organization culminates in a strict subordination of all the partial drives to the primacy of the sexual functions, which in turn are only to serve the purpose of procreation. Whatever is not tabooed is sublimated, purified, or by interpretation turned into mere auxiliary functions. Eros is no more than a merely tolerated means for the end.

Here arises an important task of the woman. Being by nature the "ingenious lover," she is able to demonstrate that a pseudo-masculine repression of eros unleashes destructive forces which otherwise would have stayed bound in the loving unifying of eros. A glance at pseudo-masculine times, nations and cultures, and their aggressive drives confirms this. Let us face it: where can the *homo faber* find a lasting defense against the advance of inhumanity when body and soul are degraded into mere instruments of procreation or into means of an unnatural, inhuman production-efficiency? *"Homo insensibilis non est homo,"* says Thomas Aquinas. Man who does away with the erotic and with all sensuality loses his humanity and becomes a robot, *l'homme machine,* an intellectual animal. This is why — as we have already seen — Russia de-eroticises movies, fashions, magazines, dances and behavior-patterns; for the body is supposed to be nothing but an instrument of an increased efficiency of production. Man and wife are not to be friends and lovers, looking into one another's face, but earth-facing comrades related in work and material.

The Hour of Woman

Thus nature becomes an object of exploitation and, at the same time, more and more loses its beauty. According to M. Nead, the "primitives," upon whom we so easily tend to look down, still call the world a garden. Garden means harmony and order, which is symbolically also expressed in the garden of paradise. In a garden rules the "and"; but in the world of unleashed intellect rules the *"contra"*: intellect *contra* nature, subject *contra* object. Eros is one of the powers of the "and"; it resists the normal degradation of its integral striving for harmony.

When we consider that today the once reviled machines provide us with more leisure time and that, because of increased specialization, working hours are constantly growing shorter, it seems to us that the very thing which once led to the repression of eros opens the possibility of giving it back its rightful place. The power of "socialization," which counteracts every separation and division, the uniting in beauty and harmony, which is a very part of eros, should once more be taken seriously. But Freud has already intimated that this historic hour of the liberation of eros can come only when the hour of the woman sounds. Naturally, this does not mean — nor do I entertain the notion — to proclaim with prophetical ardor a utopian, fanatical and certainly also false feminism. But it is certain that, if we take woman really seriously — far above the clamor for equality — we likewise do justice to the uniting power of eros. Life becomes integrated into a higher erotic order and, as a consequence, there will be fewer manifestations of a mere and brutal sexuality. When the purely genital functions of marriage are considered as a part, and not as the main part; when attitudes, gestures, words and tenderness no longer are a mistaken diversion of the drives, but a harmonious complement to them, mankind will have taken a decisive step towards its happiness.

Eros, The Power of Socialization

It seems to me that this is the only way to rediscover also the lost relationship between the I and reality. Only thus is it possible that someday the beginning and the end of mankind's history will be alike. True, the coming paradise cannot be established here. This would be the same utopia which is cherished by the communists and by certain natural scientists. But the future, gardenlike harmony can be prepared here — even more, it must be prophetically called to mind. What the "uninhibited" child — one who is not suppressed — dreams in his playful phantasy; what the "unrestrained" artists express in colors, surrealistic forms and atonal music; what the fairy tale "calls to mind" and Holy Scripture states as it awaits the lion's playing with the lamb, namely a harmony also of that which abstract intellect finds incompatible can be done through the release of eros' uniting power. Eros does not need the patriarchal superego which only arouses and intensifies guilt, nor is it a law in itself. Its law can be only the embracing agape. Then it will not be its repressed power that is a source of culture but its inherent power to fuse living substance into constantly greater and more durable unions. Then it will be the power of "socialization" which *Mater et Magistra* speaks of and which Teilhard de Chardin sees as the only possible progress towards the "Omega point."

Ubi Caritas Et Amor, Deus Ibi Est

Let us clarify this — for nothing would be more of a disservice in this matter than vagueness. What effects the actual and essential union and reunion of that which is separated by sin is agape, the love of God. Eros is not agape. But eros can and must be taken into agape, must be informed by agape. Agape is the law of eros. Eros should become permeated by spirit rather than be spiritualized. Agape should not exclude or push off eros. God's love is the "Yes."

In the liturgy of Maundy Thursday, which recently has been enriched by the washing of the feet, the choir sings in a simple melody the words which should be very much taken to heart: *"Ubi caritas et amor, Deus ibi est."* How shall we translate it? "Wherever eros and agape is, there is God"; "Wherever this and that kind of love is, there is God," or, using the apparently limited German language: "Wherever love, there is God?" *"Il n'ya pas deux amours,"* says Pascal. "There are not two kinds of love," if we only understand it right.

THE LONG, WEARISOME JOURNEY TO COMPANIONSHIP

To reach the apex where eros is incorporated into agape — an historic hour which we seem to have arrived at — mankind has traveled a long, painful journey full of thorns for the woman and for the man a tragic impairment of his nature. Even at the risk of repeating myself I would like to briefly describe this journey and to spotlight certain points. Although this description will not lead to new viewpoints it might be of help to place our problem in its historical setting and, furthermore, to learn from the mistakes of history.

1. FEAR, HATE AND THE DEVALUATION OF WOMAN

Metahistorical Fear

Already in metahistorical areas we confront myths, figures and symbols in which, according to C. G. Jung, men actually preserve the archetypes, the original forms, of their fear and fear-born hate. Ill-boding, dangerous figures are always represented as women. In the Grecian myth it is *Pandora* from whose cornucopia all evil flows in vengeance of the masculine-promethean stealing of the fire. *Omphale* turns even a Hercules, when he fell in love with her, into a clumsy figure spinning wool at her feet. *Medea's* hatred of Jason is greater than all natural motherly instincts; she kills her children in order to strike at the man. We read about *Hecuba's* terrible revenge; we see the dangerous beauty of *Helen*, for whose possession man-killing wars break out. Infatuating is the song of the sirens, enigmatic the smile of the dangerous Sphinxes. *Xanthippe,* Socrates' wife, a woman who actually existed, becomes simply the mythical versification of cantankerous and quarrelsome behavior. Thus each century has used its own feminine figures to crystallize the defense of masculine society, whether it be *Brunhild* or *Krimhild*, or the numerous figures of the late medieval fabliaux (gross jokes, popular songs), in which domineeringness and garrulity, laziness and feline cunning, coquettish vanity and many more traits are pilloried. Just as the fairy tale created the mean stepmother, the antifeminism of a Rabelais, Moliere, Schopenhauer, Mathieu and a Deschamps created the mean mother-in-law who painfully bears the brunt of the modern sideshow. Even today's enlightened scientists call hurricanes by feminine names.

Old Testamental Devaluation

In times accessible to history the notion of woman's

value and position is still in full accordance with the memory of the myths. The Jews' daily prayer was: "Blessed are you Adonai that you created me as a man and not as a woman." (Plato praises the gods with almost the same words.) And the Jew had every reason for this prayer, since the woman was surrounded by taboos and eventual uncleanness. The natural processes of birth and menstruation required long rites of purification. (Anglo-Saxons, by the way, still call menstruation "the curse.") Adultery for the woman — not for the man — was a capital crime. Woman's testimony was not valid in court. Proverbs (31) praises the woman who is never idle, who toils and moils from morning till night, while the man sits at the gate.

The peoples of Middle East surrounding Judaism had much the same attitude. Although the code of Hammurabi concedes certain rights to the woman, her life was actually very humiliating. We read, for instance, in the book of Esther that Assuerus holds a drinking-bout and sends for his wife to show her beauty to all those present. The woman refuses his request and he gets rid of her. For these peoples woman was indeed a mere commodity. Never was she allowed to address the man without being first spoken to. Even in our day, in many places of the Near East she walks several yards behind the man (except in mine-fields).

No Companionship Among The Greeks and Romans

A striking description made by Pseudodemosthenes in the fourth century B.C. tells us about the attitudes of the Greeks. Here it says: "We Hellenes have hetaeras for intellectual pleasure, concubines to satisfy our daily bodily desires, and wives for the procreation of legitimate children and as dependable housekeepers." So absorbed are we in our praise of the Greeks that too often we forget that even in the age of Pericles the woman was locked in a harem and forced to leave the education of her sons up to the gymnasium. The much praised freedom of the Greeks was as much denied to woman as it was to the slaves. By order of the man, the concubine could occupy the wife's bed. Dialogue and intellectual life flourished only in the social gatherings of often homosexual men. The emancipation of Sparta's woman can at best be called equalization; although boys and girls were given the same kind of education this by no means raised the position of the woman. Solon officially established prostitution. The prostitutes who were to have their hair tinted saffron and who were known by the cut of their clothes and the display of a red Priapus were paid a salary by the state. Roman law finally considered woman economically independent but ascribed to her *imbecillitas*, that is, weakness of the mind.

Gnostic Infiltration Into Christendom

Only with great difficulty could early Christendom free itself from the anti-feminine way of thinking. Years after their baptism Christians often still visited mystery meetings of the Gnostics. Thus we can see why the breaking loose from gnostic trains of thought turned into a gigantic intellectual struggle. The front lines have not always been clear. The Encratites and the Messalians, who sought a deliverance from the woman by the proscription of marriage, were at times considered especially pious. All the more characteristic and significant is the fact that particularly among these sects their entire life beneath the threshold became sexualized. In a similar way, centuries later, medieval Cathari, who apparently originated in the East, led a life which was at the same time both abstinent and dissolute.

The under-evaluation of the woman goes into modern times in a straight line which can be illustrated by many examples. For the man Augustine, to call the woman a "creature without backbone and firmness"; or for Bossuet, a "superfluous bone"; for Nietzsche to reserve her "for the relaxation of the warrior"; or for woman-haters, like Tolstoy, Strindberg and Schopenhauer to pour out their mockery upon her — it is all the same thing: throughout all centuries of history, behind many masks and in different garbs, this fear, hatred and the under-evaluation can be seen, rendering man incapable of doing justice to the woman and blocking every access to companionship.

Three Serious Consequences

This leads to three serious consequences. First, man becomes antagonistic to woman and in general brutal, hard and possessive. This he-man, to whom the other half of reality remains unknown and unrevealed, is a cold gripper and grasper. He has only what he can grip with his hands and grasp with his head. Secondly, many things which a true encounter with the woman could certainly have kept in a healthy balance are now effeminately shaped by the man — feminized. We observe in the Christian Churches too, that the loss of the vital polarity of the sexes, caused by the silencing of the woman, has its reaction upon the man: unmanly, sentimental traits creep into the way of speaking, into songs and devotions (possibly even into the priest's clothing [long skirts, laces]), which, in a sense, seem to justify Celsus' (second century) and Nietzsche's (nineteenth century) reproach that being a Christian makes one feminine. Over against this it is pointed out today that the Jesuits owe their great success during the seventeenth century, and their openness, to the "awakening woman." The third consequence affects the unfulfilled and unaddressed woman. Since she remains erotically undeveloped and is not taken fully seriously, she escapes, alone or in groups, into neuroses, phobias and hysterias, similar to a child who, after a little brother or sister has been born, feels neglected and escapes into an hysterical enuresis in order to reconquer the love of his parents which he believes himself deprived of. Belief in witches may have, to some extent, originated in the man's tendency to consider maidens who avoided him as witches possessed by the devil; another cause was doubtlessly the actually existing mass hysterias by which repressed femininity in an unhealthy way demanded attention.

2. THE IDOLATRY OF THE BODY

Apotheosis of the Flesh

Considering the radical rejection of the woman; considering the absolute muteness to which she is condemned by pseudo-masculine societies, the positive valuation of her body might at least seem to be a step forward. In reality, this is true only in a limited sense since the idolatry of woman's body permits only a physical encounter; and this can hardly be called a true meeting. In fact the identifying of woman with body is much more common than one usually suspects. The woman is merely expected to attract the man's desire and to let this desire end in herself. In this regard, one should examine the abstract rock-paintings in Spain, Norway and Sweden (about four to seven thousand years old), the numerous feminine idols in Mesopotamia or the Venus of Willendorf, typical of many others. They all have something in common: they represent and emphasize, in an exaggerated manner, the female sex characteristics. With this they underline the physicalness, fertility and relatedness-to-nature of the woman whom the man takes delight in, whom he conquers, possesses and enjoys. The Hottentot ideal of beauty, *Venus steatopygos*, exists even in our day. We may call to mind the Orientals' preference for fat women whose mass of flesh promise the man the purposeless luxury of voluptuousness; and the way many a modern man observes the woman, the way he evaluates her in terms of competence, or the way they talk about women among themselves, still discloses the validity of analogous or similar standards.

H. Miller's Pansexualism

In this context we might call to mind two modern writers with very different goals and artistic talents; yet they nevertheless resemble one another in their evaluation of woman as an object of man's sensual pleasure; Henry Miller and D. H. Lawrence. Henry Miller, an American who lived in Paris most of his life, boasts of having established a theory of the obscene and calls love, "what cannot be outside of the bed." A hero for him is one who can unrestrainedly dive into the "artificial eternity" of an endlessly prolonged masculine sexual ecstasy and, in his opinion, whoever emerges quickly out of this false eternity, out of this "obscene world-code" of the performing numerous consecutive sexual acts, is not a real man. As a consequence, only that woman is accepted who is not at all morally hampered from giving her body endlessly and unrestrictedly.

The "Educational Novels" of D. H. Lawrence

D. H. Lawrence speaks more clearly and in a more artistic form about a supremacy of the man which manifests itself, above all, in the physical possession of the woman. For him, sexual and phallic are identical. Woman's existence is justified only by the man, and, more exactly, only as body. Thus, in his work we can find detailed descriptions which degrade woman to a compliant slave, to a dispenser of lust for man's greed, and to a server in the temple of Phallus. Characteristically, Lawrence calls his novels educational novels since the task of the woman he depicts is to adjust to this pseudo-masculine world-picture. It is incomprehensible that in a time like ours, which, after all, is "already" talking about the equality of woman (although, as we shall see, equality cannot be the final word), opinions like Miller's and Lawrence's stand a chance to become discussable and accepted by society. Or is it that here age-old pseudo-masculinity, long since believed dead, is trying to be heard?

3. Idolatry of Womanhood

A true valuation of woman can begin only when man is willing to take seriously her difference in regard to body *and* soul. Then the polar tension is experienced not only physically but also spiritually and intellectually, and is lived in its joys and its sorrows. Through our earlier reflections on eros and agape the concept of love is so well established that we actually would prefer not to use it relative to the subject discussed here. Yet it still seems to be the most appropriate term.

A Promising Start

What we are therefore willing to call love appears first in Appollonius' *Argonautica*. There, though, it is not a moral command or an educational principle and certainly not a means of experiencing value, but it is a feeling, at times tender and at other times passionate, which often overwhelmingly pushes man and woman towards one another. Virgil's *Dido* and also *Medea* are partly based on this idea. Hellenism discovers the characteristic charm of love stories; painted as romantic idylls or pastoral scenes, they play the major part of the murals of Pompeii. (*Amor and Psyche, Hero and Leander, Daphne and Chloe*). From then on, however, until the courtly Middle Ages, this kind of love no longer plays a role, not even in the Ovidian concept according to which love is a beautiful disease which robs one's reason and paralyses the will.

Cultivation of Distance

Knighthood brings new accents. For the first time love is sensed as a happiness of the soul. This happiness of the soul is even experienced when completely independent of physical fulfillment, and is effective even in failure, and, later on, sometimes especially in failure. Also new is the feminizing tendency which courtly love bestows on the man. Woman, who was in the past the prey of the rough, plundering man, is now yearningly courted and becomes even famous for her inaccessibility and prudishness. Self-tormentingly, men analyse and manifest their longing which, being neither heard nor fulfilled, flares to unsuspected flames, while women cultivate their remoteness and distance and this all the more since in most cases they are the wives of other men, for instance the feudal lords. However one might explain this "love," whether as merely fictive or as originating in the social conditions of feudalism or as a valve of sexual repression — accessible only for depth psychology — it is certain that such cultivated love at a distance can never be the kind of love true companionship asks for. The woman of this love ritual is an ethereal being without flesh and blood. While valuated positively she nevertheless is removed into the remoteness of a myth. It is exactly the healthy physical expression of eros which these women and this love avoid. The woman sung by the troubadours as "the gate of heaven" is just as much removed from the companionship we demand today as is the woman seen by Tertullian as "the gate of hell."

False Feminism

Neither could the adulation of woman in later centuries lead to a partner-like "and" relationship to the man, but rather resulted in a false ethereal feminism. In the sixteenth century Cornelius Agrippa defends with pseudo-theological and cabalistic arguments the thesis that woman is more perfect and more virtuous than man. In the eighteenth century, Diderot and Stuart Mill made woman into an angel who seems to be not of this world. Finally we may also mention here the cliche into which modern song forces woman. She becomes the embodiment of all dreams; she is related to night, moon stars and remote shores, incapable of being met except in daydreams. The idol of this cheap sentimentality, which is the "bread" of millions of adolescents who more and more are losing the capacity for encounter, does not at all exist in flesh and blood but somewhere "in the stars." But whenever woman vanishes, man becomes stunted. Who can be surprised when he becomes first con-tactless and, in the end, simply tactless?

Don Juan's Cold War Against Woman

In the songs and everyday language of immature people certain types of men, who must be said to lack real contact with and generally also the right tact for the woman, are called "Casanovas" or "Don Juans." One uses the designations, however, without knowing their meaning — at least we can hope so. For Don Juan's veneration of the woman is actually a masquerade; basically he hates women. The proud Leporello list of the 1003 women he "possessed" is merely to prove how seducible they all are. He is never motivated by affection, not to mention love. His eroticism (if this word is not altogether out of place here) is nothing but cold war; resistance provokes him. In taking pleasure he wants to offend the woman as woman. As a matter of fact, all those seduced by him think of him as of a devil, for not one of the women he bemused with his sentimental songs was enriched by him. He leaves them behind, poisoned and humiliated, enjoying their despair with the derisive laughter immortalized by Mozart. But true eros wants to reconcile and not mock, wants to unite rather than negate.

Stendhal's Skillfulness

An awareness of this striving for union characteristic of true eros gives us a way to estimate the failure of the art of love advocated, for instance, in Stendhal's *De l'amour* and to unmask it as unerotic. Hereby we should keep in mind that this was by no means merely a kind of instruction in the art of love; many men of the nineteenth century and even of the twenties of our own century followed its doctrines. These men concentrate with ice-cold rationality on the so-called crystallization process which precedes fulfillment. Only the passion's tension is drunk to the dregs, only it is called love, while the fulfillment of the longing which, as we know, is the goal of eros, for them means its extinction. But this is pure egocentrism. Such a man does not seek the woman but rather his own physical and spiritual lust and takes sheer delight in its prolongation. It is in the nature of eros to live at distances yet, at the same time, to constantly try to overcome them. This other kind of love, however, wants to live *only* in distance: woman is expected to remain the remote being.

"Bonjour Tristesse"

Bernard of Clairvaux maintains that man is comforted only by woman. His onesidedness is balanced only by a true encounter with the woman. Thus when distance and prolongation are skillfully cultivated, the woman vanishes.

The man who experiences her only in daydreams, but who (in the biblical sense of the word) does not actually know her, becomes stunted, weakened in his ability to communicate and finally unable to love. For in reality love happens between two. Because Goethe knew this he could say more about love in four lines than do six volumes of Casanova's memoirs and the entire Leporello list. It seldom happens in our day that true love is poetically mastered. Instead, Kafka, Joyce, Proust, Becket and Sartre have articulated and given form to the lament and outcry of the soul which has become aware of its incapacity to love. Also the young Sagan in her *Bonjour Tristesse* could merely portray the absence of love.

4. The Idea of Contract

The Public Interest

The total devaluation of the woman on the one hand and, on the other, worshiping her only as body and wife make woman an object which is used and idolized. In both cases it is the man who acts and for whom the woman exists. Therefore any awareness that the woman, too, is a subject who is herself capable of acting, is certainly a positive achievement; and when we take a look at the legal position of woman within marriage from this viewpoint, the concept of the contractual character of this life-relationship can doubtlessly be called progress. The progress is not so great, however, in regard to love, which is now narrowed down into juridical terms of rights and duties. It remains uncontested, of course, that the order which the state has to guarantee, requires certain contractual securities and regulations as to the civil consequences of a marriage. What we shall discuss here is the opinion, widespread even in the Church, that the nature of marriage can be defined totally on a contractual basis. This viewpoint automatically pushes into the background the fact that marriage is two human beings in a community of love, and thus it is not surprising that the very same religions and cultures which see the procreation of offspring as the exclusive or main goal of marriage show the highest tendency to advocate the contractual character of marriage.

Sixty years ago, in Susa, Persia, a diorite pillar two meters in height was found on which the law of Hammurabi, a contemporary of Abraham, was codified in more than three-hundred paragraphs. Paragraph 128 defines marriage as a contract in which only the state is interested. Also among the Jews, marriage was not primarily a concern of two people who loved one another, but the business of the clan. The heads of families discussed, decided and married. Hence the two newlyweds did not actually start a new family but rather continued or extended the existing clan. But contracts are soluble. This was true in Hammurabi's law as well as among the Jews. Besides adultery, dislike and quarrelsomeness (Deut 21:14; Sir 25:36) were considered valid reasons for a dissolution of the contract. Similarly, in the West, marriage until very recently has been a matter of law, and its significance within the context of social order has played the main role. The objective elements of order rank higher than the subjective rules in the realm of eros and agape. Only thus can we explain why at times children have been married by their parents already in their earliest years. If later on their hearts found one another, it was a lucky chance for which they thanked God.

The Advance of Romanticism

It was only in our time that a counter-movement took place against the objective socially-bound marriage and its institutional coercion. Although Kant, in his *Fundamentals of the Metaphysics of Morals* still calls marriage a "contract of two people of different sex for the lifelong and mutual possession of their sexual properties," his definition — even though the contractual character is retained — already shows the advance of the subjective realm. No longer is mentioned the exclusive purpose of the procreation of offspring. Later on romanticism succeeded in fully grasping the meaning of marriage for the individual. It is to its credit that, for the first time, the value of woman's claim to companionship and love has been brought into consciousness. Unfortunately, it soon ran into the other extreme and considered the sufficient grounds for marriage to be, exclusively, love, while neglecting the objective order. Nevertheless, it initiated an advance into new territories, led to the discovery of basic elements of marital existence and released energies which make us indebted to romanticism. Part and parcel of this, as of every newly won freedom, is the necessity to grow and mature into a corresponding responsibility so that what has been won may unfold its worth through right use.

Penetration of Juridical Concepts Into the Church's Teaching

The *Codex Juris Canonici,* that is the code of Canon Law of the Catholic Church, in force since 1918, also treats marriage as being a contract by nature, directing its attention to the mutual "transference of the right of the body." This should not immediately lead to the conclusion that, in the thinking of Catholic theology, marriage is merely a contract. The CIC is a juridical code, and nobody expects from a juridical code anything more than the objective setting up of norms by an institution. These objectively juridical norms of the Church as such are not binding outside of its realm; they do not apply to the valid, so-called "natural marriages" of the unbaptized, nor to the marriage of two validly baptized non-Catholics. This fact alone makes it clear that the CIC itself neither can nor wants to make statements as to the full meaning of marriage. This is treated by another theological discipline: dogmatic theology oriented to scripture. Especially during the last few years, dogmatic theology has made essential contributions to the theology of marriage and to a theological basis of companionship. Nevertheless, the opinion that marriage is by nature a contract is still wide-spread among Catholics. This is partially due to misunderstanding, as many recall the filling out and signing of the so-called marriage-documents, and partially to the way marriage is presented in the talk customarily given in connection with the gospel of the wedding feast of Cana, in many dioceses. But on the other hand, this misinterpretation is also caused by an unauthorized and unjustified infiltration of juridical notions into the sphere of moral and dogmatic theology which push the positive and thus alterable legal norms into the foreground while the striving for the essential meaning of marriage recedes and grows dim. It is certainly right and good that the parishioners hear every year which marriage is valid and which is not. But just as often and with the same emphasis, we must remind Christians of the conditions for a happy marriage and try to lead them in this direction. Unfortunately, in this respect often a lack of time and of clarity leave much to be desired. Foggy religious routines are still in vogue which are actually no help for life. I say this at the risk of being corrected by many well-meaning directors of Pre-Cana conferences, and members of the Christian Family Movement. I would be happy to learn more. The "marriage instructions" of many a priest — and he's not always of the older generation — is, to put it mildly, a sad chapter.

Three Great Dangers

But let us go back once more to the notion that the nature of marriage consists in a contract. There are three reasons which should make us drop this notion. First: A contract is based on the free will of two partners. But if it comes into existence by bilateral acts of will and consists in these, then by virtue of a similar bilateral act of will this same contract can be cancelled. This is why most states consider this contracted marital relationship to be by nature dissoluble. At any rate, the indissolubility of marriage cannot be derived from its contractual character.

Second: by virtue of a contract arises a functional framework which encompasses mutual performances and transactions in which the effected contract is fulfilled. According to this only those obligations can be assumed which the partner in the contract can fully and entirely master. Now, the possibility of satisfying a marriage contract is co-determined by changes and providential occurences which lie in the future and which neither of the contracting parties can foresee. Thus, in the case of an "act of God" one or the other partner could consider himself dispensed from the contract.

Third: Contracts refer to externally comprehensible facts. But beyond these tangible and ascertainable facts there is a multitude of lines of conduct which can be in complete contradiction to the meaning of such contract. One has only to think of an "escape into an overestimated social or intellectual activity, in spiritual friendships, in religious encystment and mystic cults, in enthusiasm for great personalities, of a flight into a life of phantasy, in reading-experiences, etc. Operating in all of these can be infidelity and a latent betrayal and disloyalty to marriage, while the facade remains intact; often, in fact, it is because the marriage remains sterilely intact, and thus life is forced

to break the ties with makeshift activities" (E. Michel).
As it is, the law is "the power of the offence" (see Rom
5:20). Thus, granted that the notion of the contractual
character of marriage is progress, it is not sufficient and
can even be dangerous, once we view the heights of the
marital "and" relationship, towards which man and woman
must be led. We should, above all, keep in mind that, although regulations of Canon Law — which the Church as
visible community cannot do without — are based on and in
intimately organic connection with Catholic theology, they
cannot fully express or substantially exhaust this theology.

5. EQUALITY

Confrontation of Man and Woman

The demanded equality, too, corresponds to a still pre-
vailing juridical way of thinking. In the so-called emancipation movement man and woman are contrasted with
each other like two autonomous, rounded-off individuals.
This causes a strong temptation to formulate the question
rising in the struggle over legal positions: man *or* woman,
and to overlook the conquering of the differences through
the relatedness of man *and* woman to one another. Whoever has eyes to see and ears to hear will soon recognize
that many male and female "combatants" succumb to
this danger and thus separate "what God has united."
Such separation, however, means endless alienation, fight-
ing, and working against one another.

Actually, the woman's struggle for equality with the man
and for her acceptance as partner is quite understandable.
We have only to call to mind the above sketched historical
frame of reference. Nevertheless, before our understanding
turns into sympathy we must recognize the danger that the
problem, which hitherto was seen only onesidely through the

eyes of the man, is now seen, just as onesidedly, through the eyes of woman. As it stands, this danger is already present in the wrong formulation of the question as such, which, as a consequence, can only lead to a wrong answer. Positive legal regulations on the part of the state will always be a matter of necessity; they can also create a sort of precondition, a certain climate, in which the man and the woman can move safely; but, by themselves, they provide neither help nor security for the essentials of the marital "and" relationship.

Of what value is it for woman to be admitted to a university, to have an active and passive right to vote, equal payment for equal work and many other things which can be legally regulated and secured, when she, in spite of all this, is merely the "or" of humanity? What good is there in the fight for power and the striving for independence, when it leads to a disillusioning materialization of all relationships between man and woman, including the sexual and the erotic? When the so-called liberation of woman (a treacherous phrase) brings nothing better than the separation of the woman from the man, a disservice has been rendered to both.

We should not confuse things. One of woman's slogans in the "war of liberation" was the battle-cry: freedom of profession. Today, after but a few years of economic development, hardly anyone talks any longer about freedom of profession, but many women are already under the thumb of these professions. The freedom, longed for as an ideal, has actually become a political or economic necessity. The woman, whose realm of life, according to Schelsky, is the "primary social relationship" (that is, the house, the husband, the children) is thrown into abstract social relationships, which really constitute the man's world and realm of life, and there can be no doubt that this puts her in the danger of alienating herself from her natural womanhood, and of losing her unifying power. In the materialized relationships, where dry calculation and bureaucratic publicity prevail, she will only seldom find an opportunity to prove her polarizing power and to use her capacity of devotion. Moreover, she divests herself, to a great extent, of the man's gentlemanly protection and of a certain consideration demanded by her nature.

Hierarchical Structure

Thus when we called the fight for equality a wrong or inadequate way of formulating the questions, which consequently must lead to wrong answers, this does not imply the so often voiced opinion that Catholic theology is an enemy of this equality. This equality is simply not of primary interest to her. Inasmuch and insofar as this is a purely juridical or sociological question, the Church therefore leaves its solution up to the jurists and sociologists. In regard to the essentials of marital companionship, however, the theologian orientates himself towards Holy Scripture, in which marriage and the relationship of the sexes are hierarchically structured. This follows in particular from those parts of scripture which emphasize the man's headship over the woman. 1 Peter 3:1-6 underlines the "professional obligation" of the wife to adapt to the hierarchical order, and in the rules for the Christian home (Col 3:18; Eph 5:22-23) St. Paul stresses the same thought. This hierarchical structure of marriage is simply connected with its nature and only marginally touches the juridical part. For through the nature of the sexes God himself has revealed the coordination of man and woman, and the hierarchical relationship of the spouses, and has transmitted it to us figuratively in the account of the creation of Adam and Eve. After all it seems significant that Genesis in regard to subhuman creatures, does not speak of a separate and different creation of the two sexes; a fact which rightly leads to the conclusion that the temporal priority of Adam's creation mysteriously indicates his superiority in the hierarchical order of the relationship of the sexes. Moreover God's consideration before creating the first woman makes it evident that she was created "for the man's sake," wherefore Paul calls woman "the glory of the man" (1 Cor 11:7), just as Adam called his wife "wo-man."

Mysterium Unitatis

Once more let us recall here that these deliberations focusing on the natural relatedness of the sexes, have nothing to do with the juridical problems concerning the pros and cons of equality. Besides we could easily confront those places of Holy Scripture which emphasize man's priority with others which seem to buttress the idea of equality. Thus Paul, 1 Cor 7, repeated in regard to the woman almost word for word what he said about the man. In Gal 4:28 is expressly stated that "in Christ are neither male nor female," which means the same as "neither is man independent of woman nor woman independent of man in the Lord" (1 Cor 11:11). Such passages from scripture when correctly interpreted, can contribute more to the question of equality than all jurists, blue stockings and antifeminists have ever done.

But when we see the total picture of the scriptural references concerning our problem, and above all when we correctly understand the point of view of the account of creation, we must arrive at the conviction that woman certainly was not formed out of man in order to prove some kind of formal equivalence from which the so-called equality could be derived. The high point of the entire account of creation seems rather to be this solemn "therefore"

(Gen 2:24) which no longer reports but which explains the meaning and which points to the oneness, to the *mysterium unitatis*. This "therefore" means: *because* the woman is taken from the man and is thus his glory; *because* she is the wo-man, man *and* woman can become that unity which is called the "becoming-one-flesh." This copula is, as we know, of a different kind from any existing in the world of animals, of two equivalent and equal, merely sexually differentiated parts of a pair. It is the high point and incorporation of "knowing" in oneness, which is possible only within the hierarchical structure. Thus the hierarchical origin is the creation-base and the natural foundation of the "and" relationship between man and woman, modeled by God after the relationship between the head and the body. In this context, the hierarchical coordination plays an insignificant role in the realization of the marital community of the *body*. But it will be important in the formation of the community of *life*, inasmuch as, because of their innate dispositions, the external formation is reserved more for the man and the inner realm of marriage more for the woman.

In conclusion we state that Holy Scripture neither lets itself become a leader of equality nor does it "obstinately and backwardly" fight it. Scripture sees between man and woman not a relationship of symmetry, but the coordination of something dissimilar by which both can find their way (back) to the happiness of oneness.

COMPANIONSHIP

Woman's Demand of Intellect

It seems to me that our time, in particular, needs to recognize the necessity of companionship and the way to live this companionship according to its nature. Far too long have we known but two forms of feminine life: the virgin and the mother. Hardly or not at all did man know the companion whom he needs and who helps him find happiness and contentment. Yet this simultaneously caused important powers within woman to be stunted, and entire spiritual areas remained uncultivated and undeveloped. For femininity, in particular, longs for the "and" relationship of partnership. Being closely connected with nature and its powers, woman bears in herself the longing for the man's freeing intellect and she wants it to be brought into the marital dialogue. Consequently it is the man's task not to exclude his intellect from the marital conversation but to bring it in entirely. True, woman can today participate in the facts and events of life freely and almost as naturally as the man. But she nevertheless wishes man to explain to her the new complexities of life and to order them into a coordinated scale of established values. As a matter of fact, numerous inquiries among women show that they desire, above all, a man who is intellectually superior. And — especially since the merely institutionally superior man to-day has been left without the crutches of the institution — they look all the more for the man who is in fact superior.

Intellectualizing, A Danger

This natural demand of the woman for the intellect is the exact contrary of a false intellectualizing which, in the last analysis, is detrimental both to herself and marriage. The emancipation movement often looked for its salvation in this direction and masculinized and uprooted the woman. The goal of her intellectual needs should rather be the striving to bring the masculine intellect, which so easily drifts in aridity and in areas alienated from life, back again and again into the proximity of real life.

According to this, woman's intellectual aspiration should not venture to such a "height" that, because of it, the physical encounter is felt as humiliating. In marriage one should not see the sexual sphere merely under biological aspects which, as is contemptuously said, man has in common with the animal. Thus when the woman, for such reasons, "performs" the sexual "giving of herself" merely as an "embarrassing duty" which, unfortunately, "is part of it," anxiety and frigidity are almost necessary consequences. It is of little use when unenlightened psychotherapists try to render such anxious and frigid women sexually capable (as they call it), that is, to further add sexual momentum to a sometimes "virtuous," sometimes hypersensitively untouchable pseudo-spirituality. This only makes the damage, which had its root in entirely different areas, completely irreparable.

Union of The Body

Let us reject, also in light of the above deliberations, the term "sexual intercourse." This word has something punctual in it. Rather we should speak about a "community of the body"; for, as we know, this is a matter of mutual unfolding, of unraveling individual mysteries of life for the sake of a new *One*. Sexual union has its meaning exclusively in the context of an all-embracing total unfolding. Then, however, it is one of the high points of their life together, and therefore natural considerateness, attentiveness and tenderness and the "almost meticulous soul-body sensitivity to one another" (E. Michel) should also always push and lead in this direction and prepare this apex of "becoming-one-flesh." Women in particular need this long, patient soul-body preparation and without it generally find it impossible to give themselves totally.

It would be frivolous therefore to put aside or "treat" as "sexual frailty" the need of such very individual forms of sexual experience which is the woman's contribution to the physical union. It is rather that these very forms lead the man away from a brutal taking-possession of her and teach him to become through patience and consideration a reverent listener to her individual mysteries. As a matter of fact, many marriages break apart in the brutal initiation rites of the wedding night which plays so big a role in the jokes of wedding parties and in the nightmares of innocent girls. This is the reason why modern psychotherapists go back to the advice, which more sensitive times followed without scientific encouragement, to observe the so-called "Tobias-nights" (Tob 6:18-22). It demands of the man patience and a truly loving waiting, which alone enable the woman after days — and then spontaneously — to unfold herself. This advice is buttressed by physiologists who teach us that the genital organs of the woman — in contrast to man's — are not erogenous, that is, spontaneously pleasure giving, but become so only gradually in a loving total devotion. The joyful experience of orgasm which many a woman is deprived of through her entire life (even though she may have borne ten children) often depends on this total devotion which is to be awakened in loving patience and fulfilled in reverence for the other.

Marital "Duty"

We have just noted that the capability of conception and the capability of orgasm are two completely different things and entirely independent of one another. Hence for total devotion it is not sufficient to "perform the marital duty," as juridical language calls it, with a more or less indifferent attitude. Depth psychologists have long since recognized that in cases where rights are demanded and obligations fulfilled, this demanding and performing is only seldom the expression of total devotion. A "sexual intercourse" based on such motivations easily, and unfortunately very often, serves "different kinds of unconscious motives like vengance, retaliation, compensation for various inferiority complexes, fear and defiance" (Michel) and many other forms of unsolved conflict situations of the life of the individual, which "convert into the sexual." The sexual is used as a means or a form of covering up, and the speaking in terms of rights and obligations is a handy way to do it. In summary we might say that the sexual encounter always takes place within the context of a deeper meaning. It is in the service of influential powers which express themselves in it. These powers should and can be the powers of love; yet they can also be something inferior — even vulgar.

Performance in Wholeness

As we can see, it is of utmost importance to cultivate, humanize and civilize sexual life. Marital union should not demand "efforts" of the woman but should allow her a spontaneous, free, integral participation of her whole person. She is not only the object to whom something happens and who is dealt with, but also the subject who herself gives and takes. Only so is union achieved. This means that woman's nature forces the man to "let it cost himself more", so that the happiness may also be a two-in-one. The virtue of chastity has before and after marriage a completely different aspect than within marriage. Both before and after marriage it is permissible to see in chastity the ethical perfection of the individual and for the individual in sexual matters. But every reflection on marital chastity must, necessarily and according to its meaning, be based on two-in-one-ness; it must, after centuries of individualisticly narrowed concepts of virtue, be rediscovered and courageously taught. The more the woman succeeds in asserting her nature and its properties within the partnership of marriage, the more will it be possible to mold a sexual life out of the power of chaste love.

Teacher of Love

Then the man will be once more, to say it with Goethe, "educated through the woman." Only through her can he be freed from his autistic striving for possession and pleasure, and through a patient and chastely loving coordination to the woman, find for himself a new way to mankind in general. Indeed, hardly anybody can deny that men tend to be somewhat primitive in sexual matters; the man is seldom the ingenious lover in marriage. Age-old are masculine prejudices, the recollection of "fundamental patriarchal rights", which make it so difficult for the man to give up his somewhat brutal tendencies. In most cases, therefore, the woman can learn very little from him in regard to true expressions of love— by which we do not mean here physical manipulation and skill. But what man can learn from woman is what concerns the prerequisites and the center of their life together and of companionship.

Thus, not without reason the man instinctively expects the woman to know what love is, to know its possibilities and forms of expression. This means that we must abandon the false concept of chastity as it used to be extolled in sermons, books of devotion and by well-meaning mothers who confused this valuable virtue with ignorance in matters of love. Otherwise the man, who himself, too, was obligated to this premarital chastity, would be the only "teacher" of love and his "initiation" would onesidedly set the pattern for both. Often an open or secret anxiety and a permanent bad conscience are the consequences. But when the man, who hitherto was completely absorbed in the abstract and in pure objectivity, also feels and fears his ineptitude in ways of expressing love, they both will, in order to find a solution, resort to some of the hundreds of "instructions in the art of love" which are available today. Actually, these instructions in themselves cannot be offhandedly condemned. If they are truly respectfully informative and are woven into marital life at the right time, they can be definitively useful. But it is high time that a greater number of sincere, well-informed people, encouraged by the Church, get a hearing. Otherwise we have no reason to complain that the gates remain wide open for the teaching of purely artificial skills, and that such isolated techniques and practiques rather hinder than foster marital union. A survey of men showed that most of them find "fantasy" in love lacking in their wives. Since they long ago admitted their own incapability, they expect the woman they love to have a certain healthy experience quite compatible with innocence, which she brings into the becoming-one of marriage.

The Nature of Marital Chastity

Because of its importance we come back once more to the question of chastity and unchastity, for it cannot be overlooked that different opinions are held in this matter. The examination of conscience in our prayer books and the premarital instructions generally put paramount emphasis, as has already been said, on the "naturality" of marital intercourse. By this is meant its principal aptness, measured by exterior standards, to procreate offspring. We, on the other hand, have emphasized as most important the two-in-one-ness of husband and wife into which, and, more precisely, in an ordered, integral way, both masculine intellect and woman's body are to be brought. The physical union should be an expression of that all-encompassing love which finds peace and happiness only in the becoming-one-flesh which in this life represents the highest possible form of "knowing," of experiencing one another. Our reasoning is biblical. Eve was created for the sake of this union. For her sake, man leaves father and mother. The children are the blessing which God has joined to this uniting event. Everyday experience confirms this biblical foundation. Neither in the entering of a marriage nor in marital-sexual union does the idea of offspring play the paramount role. The man and the woman marry and come together because they love each other. In this love, they wish to give themselves to one another, and to receive from one another; want to form their inner life and lead to maturity. Within the expression of this love procreation is *one* possibility. Hence the chastity of marriage refers, first of all, to the wholeness of the love and cannot primarily be connected with the possibility of propagation included in it.

Wrong Purposive Thinking

We still find people who consider sexual desire permissible only when transformed into the conscious intention of procreating children. Such morality is absurd and based on a complete misunderstanding of biblical and psychological facts. The depth psychologist may uncover this demand as a secret, non-integrated remnant of suspicion of sex. Another factor may be the unadmitted idea that man's sexuality, if its acceptance and expression cannot be avoided, should at least serve a "sublime," that is, one higher than itself, purpose. Thus they even "outdo" St. Paul who certainly cannot be called lax, and Peter, the prince of the Apostles. In 1 Cor 7:3, physical union of the spouses is not seen from the viewpoint of procreation, but is called a "debitum" which both spouses owe to one another. The so-called procreative purpose is not what sets the limit, but the at times necessary leisure for prayer. Peter's first letter deals with the problem in a similar way. "Dwell with your wives considerately" (1 Pet 3:7), which probably means the same thing as, live in awareness of the mystery of becoming-one, expressed in sexual union. Obviously the Apostles did not hold to the argumentation of the rigorists in matters of marital chastity.

At the same time this rigorous attitude also appears more pious: whenever the sexual is subordinated to the purpose of procreation, or in other words, when the wrong purpose is assigned to it, the procreator is easily understood to be the cause of the child and the child the necessary effect. Certainly nobody denies a certain causative relationship between sexual union and conception. Neither does scripture deny this. But it is necessary to preserve reverence for the mystery of fecundation and to emphasize the gratefulness for God's blessing. "Be fruitful and multiply" (Gen 1:28) can never be a command. If it were, conception and birth would have to be within man's power. Rather these words are a blessing and any other interpretation is profound disbelief. Moreover, in passing, let us mention that, at first, Adam calls his wife "woman" (the one taken from man and tending towards him). Only later when after the loss of paradise his life is menaced by death, does he call her "Eve," that is, mother of life. But it is the very Catholic idea that original sin did not totally destroy man's nature but only affected the blessing of fertility in that from now on it is combined with the pains of birth.

Community of Life

Let us also recall that there are marriages which, according to God's will, remain without children and, in spite of this, are complete marriages. Likewise marriages with children already grown up, are not dead monuments of the past but continue to be vital because the task of mutual unfolding and deciphering each other remains now as before. For the becoming-one-body is not a task given only for the most vital time of life but also for the abating and extinguishing periods. Even the cautious encyclical *Casti connubii*, referring to the *Catechismus Romanus* (II, VIII, 13) says expressly that one can "very truly and rightly call the mutual inner formation of the spouses, and the persistent striving to lead one another to perfection, the main purpose and actual meaning of marriage." But in this case marriage must not be seen in the narrow sense of a mere purposive community of procreation and education of children, but its full sense as a community of life.

"Frustratio Seminis"

One reason why the rigorists were often unable to grasp the nature of chastity and unchastity was their preoccupation with the concept of *"frustratio seminis"*: that the useless wasting of man's sperm is the basis of the sin. But this idea, which was of great importance in the history of moral theology, is founded on a line of thought long obsolete and proven to be incorrect. The peoples of antiquity and of the Orient, for instance, because of their basic patriarchal attitude, believed man's sperm to be something sacred, something divine. Other peoples and also the Middle Ages believed man's sperm to be the only active element in the propagation of the human race. And since, on the one hand, the hard struggle for existence demanded as many children as possible and, on the other hand, the high mortality rate of children was a threat to this demand, needless wasting of this important masculine substance had to be punished. Today we know more about propagation. Matter-form thinking no longer blurs our vision. Besides, because of the diminishing mortality of the newborn and children, we can expect almost all of them to reach adult-hood, a fact which leads rather to the problem in reverse, namely, whether in view of the feeding of the world population an excessively large number of children still seems reasonable. Besides, we are more and better informed as to the physiological processes of sexual union and know that in every union a *"frustratio seminis"* takes place, since of the hundreds of thousands of sperm ejaculated one alone is needed and used for conception. (The remaining "unnecessary" sperm aids woman in liberating the powers of companionship.) Moreover, since conception itself is entirely independent of man's will, and since not every conjugal act causes or can cause fertilization, it seems to be clearly God's will, revealed in such way by nature, that the marital union may take place more often and in spite of this, or better, for this very reason, remain meaningful. Also in those cases where it is absolutely certain that for physiological reasons offspring cannot be procreated, but where nevertheless a complete union takes place, the dogmatic theologian supposes an increase of sanctifying and helping grace within the spouses, and this by virtue of the body-soul union in love. In cases of an already existing pregnancy during the nursing period, in the infertile period, in advanced age or after certain kinds of surgery, the meaning of the marital community of body and love is not only preserved but should continue to be realized. All these reasons it seems to me, should cause us to thoroughly think over once more the meaning of chastity and unchastity. The problem of conscious and responsible motherhood, which is part of this, will be taken up in the last chapter.

Novitiate of Companionship

The appropriate time to frankly discuss this question without prudishness or false pathos is the time of the "great novitiate" of marriage, the period of engagement. Unfortunately the education of the woman who as the "ingenious lover" is more qualified to be the teacher of love, leaves, as already mentioned, much to be desired. The modern economic structure demands a very differentiated education of the girl and adolescent young woman which requires a disproportionately long period of time. These women go for years through a very specialized training for a profession soon to be abandoned and by many of them considered temporary even at the start. Yet for their proper goal of becoming a wife and a mother they often are without any kind of preparation. The result is what we see every day; for what is decisive for the happiness or unhappiness of a marriage is not so much the excellent training of bookkeepers or of stewardesses as is the knowledge of the body-soul prerequisites for marriage and of the mysteries and greatness of true love.

Up to the end of the Middle Ages, many convents of women provided the necessary educational preparation of the girl unaffectedly and in the best sense of the word. Today, in addition to the parents and the Church, good schools and women's associations have to assume this educational task. It is not only a matter of activating woman for professional and public work, to imbue her with the capacity of handling 80 percent of the nation's wealth; it is also — and above all — a question of teaching her creative companionship. Professional life makes heavy demands on today's young women; but this — sad — situation cannot permit a justification of the fact that the already proverbial unstableness of marriages is caused by a psychologically poor preparation or by no preparation at all.

Marriage Instruction

According to canon 1020 of the CIC the Catholic priest is obliged to make a so-called premarital investigation.

This is a preliminary inquiry as to the permissibility of the intended marriage; possible impediments are to be discovered or eliminated. Furthermore, an investigation of a true marriage intention and of religious knowledge is requested. In the marriage instruction following this inquiry, the engaged couple is to be informed as to the sacred character of marriage and exhorted to receive the sacraments before marrying. Thus here as well as in many already established discussion groups for engaged couples, we have already a framework which allows the Church to establish a thorough novitiate of marriage and to make possible an open consideration of essentials.

Three Educational Goals

Here we must keep in mind three educational goals. First, girls should be freed from any dull sense of inferiority, from any uneasiness in regards to the value and rank of her femininity. Secondly, many obsolete, nonsensical educational principles which hinder the affective development of the girl must be abolished; for often the most primitive taboos defying every principle of natural and also of revealed ethics are given the honorable name of morality. A healthy valuation of the sexual must loosen up tensions and finally eliminate the "foreign bodies" which have infiltrated into Christendom from the outside. The third demand is closely connected with this: the marriage instruction should not so much be a moralizing one but a religious orientation in which chastity, too, has a more meaningful place. It is especially important that the girl, in particular, become free from illusionary fantasies of "types," and that the projections of false ideals from the world of movies and sport, which render a marital encounter with a real person with his light and dark sides difficult or impossible, be rectified or eliminated. Marriage is neither one great feast nor mere misery and torture. In a good family atmosphere, many a problem will find a natural solution; but in cases where this atmosphere is shallow, foggy or confused, marriage instruction will be imperative. Only when we succeed in placing in the foreground the true meaning of the marital community instead of its purposive aspect; only when we succeed in leading to an understanding of true two-in-one companionship, will the brittleness and frailty of many modern marriages find its prophylactic treatment.

"Knowing" Theologians

Perhaps these views are asking too much of priests. For more than a thousand years they have kept theology within the Church exclusively for themselves. The same priests have been more than a thousand years unmarried. Therefore they necessarily lack the intimate experience of the sexual two-in-oneness, for sexual knowledge cannot be acquired and increased as can other kinds of knowledge. There may be sciences and insights which can be acquired in the abstract, but the mystery of the sexual is certainly not experienced in this way. Therefore, in its final meaning it must remain alien to a celibate cleric, even though incisive argument might maintain the contrary. The onesided concern with purpose, from the point of view of pure finality, is indeed proof of this typically masculine-theoretical way of thinking. Fortunately for our day, theology is no longer guardedly reserved for the priests but also successfully "dealt with" by laymen. This may be one of the reasons why today a theology of marriage is developing which, for a change, does not deal exclusively with the family but with marriage itself, its nature and the sacramental blessing of the sexual. It is the lay-theologian who is concerned with the developmental understanding of the sexual mystery — not simply also and in passing, but weaving it inextricably into the sacramental marriage. Their own marriage provides the experience that the sexual is a powerful means of expressing love and that consequently this sexuality need not be scantily and bashfully covered but that in it the community of body and love is raised into the grace of God. Therefore they refuse the idealistic superstructure which has been so often moralizingly erected. It is my hope and desire that these "knowledgeable" theologians will give the kind of marital instruction which our time so much needs.

EXAMPLES AND MODELS OF COMPANIONSHIP

Model and personification of the virgin is Mary. She is also the image of true motherhood. Matthias Gruenewald, the theological painter, represented both sides of her womanhood with unique tenderness and beauty in his "Madonna of Stuppach." In this painting, one — the virginal — hand of the mother of God wears the nuptial ring (which finds its counterpart in the little chain of the bridegroom on the arm of her child who is God), while the other hand protects and guards the child with motherly warmth. Far from any sentimental exploitation and cheap sweetness, Mary's virginal-mother mystery is here represented in austerely beautiful originality. Yet Mary is not a model of marital companionship in the sense explained in this work. Her relationship to Joseph, the "bridegroom," the foster-father of Jesus, was of a kind other than sexual and did not comprise the inner area of eros and agape which is the basic law of the conjugal "and" relationship.

The So-Called "Joseph" Marriage — Not A Model

Our seeking of saintly models canonized by the Church meets real difficulty when we study the biographies of canonized married men and women. Besides the fact that in many cases they are historically unfounded and must first be pulled out of an overgrowth of scrub, they often tell more about the sexual attitudes of the times than about the marital relationship of these saints. Chastity is "extolled" as negative abstinence from all sexuality. The woman's virtuousness often consists in a kind of continuous martyrdom of living together with a brutal man. In the *Commune Sanctorum* of the Masses for Saints, we have Masses for virgins and martyrs. Wives go only under the name "non-virgins." Especially praised are those marriages in which both husband and wife, for supernatural reasons, observe complete sexual abstinence. This kind of relationship between man and wife, in Germany called Joseph-marriages, are from the legal as well as from the human viewpoint so problematical that they can hardly be presented as valid models for married people (for example the marriage between St. Pulcheria and St. Marcianus, and between the German emperor Henry I and his wife Cunegunda).

Difficulty of Canonization

Surely the Church has already given birth to holy wives and companions who became saints, not in spite of, but because of, their relationship to their husband. As we know, with canonization the Church intends to single out from "the great number nobody can count" those saints who through their example seem to be a remedy for a specific time. Certainly our time is in great need of a saintly woman and companion and it would be good if the Church could meet this need by canonizing one.

However, there is a great difficulty which we should not fail to recognize. In a true union, the spiritual and physical becoming-one of two loving spouses screens itself against the outside and allows no glance into its beginning, its growing, its sufferings and its happiness. Everyone, consequently any third person, is unauthorized and access is forbidden. Therefore, in the process necessary for canonization, it is difficult to gather documentary evidence of occurrences, experiences, and so on, which by their very nature shun any kind of publicity. And yet what would have to be pointed to as the basic root of sanctity are the uniting high points of this "two-in-one flame" (L. Bloy). Thus, having only an outsider's view, we will have to be satisfied with cautious allusions and suppositions.

Poetic Portrayal

Poetic representation and portrayal of companionship is superior to documentary description, since by using form and imagery it can show and make visible what in actual life tact and modesty hide from sight and publicity. In some sense the poet's figures are even more real than reality, since reality becomes transparent in a poetic creation. Since the poet is able, in such manner, to lift the veil which life does not lift, our request to Christian poets is that they present to us valid figures of a woman-companion flowering in eros-agape.

Paul Claudel, in several of his plays, has already portrayed the mysterious relationship between man and woman whose cross consists in bridging the distances from which this relationship actually lives. True, in his *Satin Slipper*, this profoundly theological poet does not present us with a companionship in the above mentioned sense. But — to my knowledge for the first time in Christian world literature — we find in the figures of Donna Proeza and Rodrigo the idea of the connection between eros and the cross, an idea with which I would like to conclude this chapter. Woman is a savior for man, is the one who awakens him to life. Through her, man sets out to search, starts on his way. But woman remains a *promise* — at least during this life. *Fulfillment* is granted to man only when the flame of love, enkindled here, glows over into the eternal. The distance which, in spite of all ardent desires, manifests itself time and again after the conjugal union, is the sword which the lovers stick into each other's heart. But this sword teaches them how to give up one another in God. The poet who calls woman a "burning star in the storm of the Holy Spirit" teaches us the lofty lesson that the Holy Spirit effects union by burning away all earthly dross and eliminating those distances which are more painfully experienced the greater the love. The nostalgia which here arises will be fulfilled only in heaven. There the uniting act of the Holy Spirit will be completely effected. Spirit-ual women, who in their love for the husband can let him sense that eros and cross belong together, are the true "teachers of love." They "promise" only as much as they, "here," are able to give.

Chapter 4

THE HOLY SPIRIT
AND WOMAN ARE
LIFE-GIVERS

THE LIFE-GIVING POWERS

The Divine Streams of Life

Let us cast a glance back. We described the analogy between the Holy Spirit and woman first with the negative statement that both are nameless. From this we drew the conclusion that coordination is proper to their nature, and from this positive definition of their being, came to see that the Holy Spirit and woman are, for one thing, the great recipients and, for another thing, the great uniters. In other words: they incorporate the power of a constant openness towards the other, and the power of union. As to woman, these powers are concretized in virginal preparedness for God and in companionship with the man. There remains still a third, mentioned already in our introduction: the relationship to the child and to everything in need.

We know already that "love" is the name proper to the Holy Spirit. In this personal love Father and Son are united in community; yet this love does not remain closed within itself, it goes out from God in the person of the Holy Spirit. The quality of giving themselves refers to all three persons; but it especially corresponds, in a mysterious way, to the actual nature of the Holy Spirit. He visibly or invisibly continues the mystery of his eternal origin through his temporal mission. Through him, men receive supernatural life. Through his indwelling, grace and sonship are given. By the communication of the Spirit, the non-divine creature is, we can say, taken into the life of the three-fold God.

Even those theologians who reject the personality of the Holy Spirit, or who give it a modalistic twist, speak of him always as God's effective power, as God's perpetual giving to his creation. They agree that the Holy Spirit is the great overflow of God's life. Through him, God bends towards his creation. Thus we read (Wisd 1:7) that the Spirit of the Lord fills the world, is all-embracing. The prophet Joel says (3:1-5) that "afterwards" this spirit will be poured out upon all mankind; which Peter referred to in his sermon on the first Pentecost (Apoc 2:16). In Ezechiel's great vision it is God's spirit who brings the dead bones to life (37:1-14). We could multiply these references. God's spirit comes upon the virgin, he overshadows her and awakens within her the life of the savior (Luke 1:35). "As a dove" he descends upon the baptism in the Jordan (Matt 3:16); in violent wind and fire, he gives himself to the Apostles at the first Pentecost (Acts 2:2-3). All these are manifestations in which his giving and working becomes clearly evident.

The "Sober Drunkenness"

When speaking about the "spirit that gives life" (John 6:64), scripture likes to use the image of pouring, of giving to drink, and of flowing. "The charity of God is poured forth in our hearts by the Holy Spirit" (Rom 5:5). The same image is used in the letter to Titus (3:6). In 1 Cor 12:13 we read about the Spirit given us to drink, and Ephesians 5:18 asks directly to be "filled with the Spirit" — indeed some witnesses of the first Pentecost actually thought the Apostles "full of new wine" (Acts 2:13). Perhaps we may even be tempted to think that the "fountain of the water of life," from which to him who thirsts will be given "freely" (Apoc 21:6), is the streams of life within the Holy Spirit flowing on a new mankind.

Spirit and Life

The great theologians take the stand of Holy Scripture clearly and unmistakably. Duns Scotus asks: "How can anyone call the Holy Spirit sterile since he is actually God's fertility?" Thomas Aquinas points out that our Creed calls the Holy Spirit the giver of life, and reminds us of the living breath from which comes also the physical life of sensate beings, and thus of the intimate relationship between spirit and life.

When, as is evident, the second account of creation (Gen 2:7 ff), which is strongly anthropomorphic, says that Yahweh breathed his breath, and hereby life, into man, this seems to mean two different things: first, that human life did not develop "simply" out of some kind of pre-existent forms, but through the mediation of the divine breath of Spirit; and secondly, that even man's natural life is, in a mysterious way, united with the divine.

Therefore it also says conversely that, if God's spirit would be withdrawn, all flesh would perish together (Job 34:14; Ps 104:29). The New Testament hardly differs from this notion. To possess the divine pneuma means life, to lose it, death. In places like Matt 27:50; Luke 23:46; John 19:30; Acts 7:59; James 2:26, this becomes very evident. Thus we can understand that the earliest theologians speak about God's Spirit hovering over the graves of the dead, sustaining, as it were, the union between body and soul, and, at the resurrection, returning to the body. The New Testament concept of pneuma is in many instances so close to our notion of the soul that one can arrive at the conclusion that God's pneuma and the principle of life are one and the same. This pneuma, this spirit of God, is what vivifies everything, what brings everything to life, to the natural as well as to the supernatural. Every birth and rebirth happens in the sign and through the power of the Holy Spirit. But this love streams down and makes fertile, only when humility, openness, awareness of our own imperfection, and admission of our smallness and weakness, open the gates here on earth and prepare the way. Promethean pride, ingrained selfsatisfaction and autarchic confidence in one's own power, are therefore the real sins against the Holy Spirit.

The Paraclete

The Holy Spirit is also called paraclete, which means the one who is called to aid, the helper, the comforter. In him, God bends towards mankind crying for help. "Like a mother comforts her little child, so will I comfort you" says Isaiah (66:13), and Jesus might have been thinking of this when he compared himself to the protecting hen which gathers her young (Matt 23:37). The Holy Spirit not only gives life, not only pours it out, but he also preserves and shelters it in a motherly way.

Spirit of Freedom

"Where the spirit of the Lord is, there is freedom" (2 Cor 3:17). According to Paul, the flesh and the law are coordinated to one another just as, on the other side, spirit and freedom demand one another. For grace, which is the indwelling of the Holy Spirit, disempowers the law (see Rom 6:14) and effects the freedom of the children of God. Whatever the spirit binds in love, he simultaneously releases into freedom. Augustine therefore says: "Love and do what you will." One who is bound in love to God and fellow man is always one who is released into freedom.

The Holy Spirit and Woman Give Birth

These considerations confirm another analogy between the Holy Spirit and woman, namely the typically motherly *giving and endowing,* the sheltering and the *releasing-into-freedom.*

The Eastern Church sings of Mary: "You gave birth to the son without father, to the son who was born by the father without mother." In these few words of the hymn glows the intimate relationship between two mysteries: "The Holy Spirit is not the representative of the Father but he creates the condition, the state of motherliness as a spiritual power of giving birth, as a multiplication of being" (Evdokimov). Thus woman's motherliness reveals itself in her ontic union with the Holy Spirit. He who "brings forth" by the power and order of the Father, is reflected in every physical and spiritual "delivery," which is what determines the nature of human motherliness.

THE NATURE OF MOTHERLINESS

Mother of Life

The general theme of the life of every motherly woman could be put into the words inscribed in a fountain in South Germany: "To give, to give, always and ever to give — that is my life." Time and again we find in the myths of all peoples, in age-old pictures and symbols, this idea of the woman as the always-giving and life-instilling mother. Up to the beginning of the more advanced cultures, she is equated with the fertile earth, from whose "motherly womb" all life springs and arises. Islamism has the same idea in calling woman the "field of the man." Greek tales of the great Gaea, the All-mother, and their representations of Diana of Ephesus with her many breasts expressing fertility, remind us of the age-old idea of equating woman with the earth in view of the fertility of both. In all cultures and at all times forms of womanhood have been represented as the norm. The oldest and most frequently found norm is fertile motherliness. Therefore cultic tradition of the earliest peoples in historical times knows of curative plants for infertility, has magic and astrological exercises to force fertility, and blessings of the bridal bed for its increase. Woman's task is to be "the mother of life" (Gen 3:20), and it is but a consequent expansion of this idea that, according to the ancients, man at his death returns to the mothers. The mother gave the life and it is she to whom it returns (see Sir 40:1).

United to Life

Thus the motherly woman, by nature, is united to life. The man is in constant danger of detaching and alienating from life, of analysing and separating. Not even the dignity of his fellowman can stop him; he inflicts wounds upon wounds and is not afraid of sowing misery and death for some "high" (life despising) goals. Therefore the phrase "without any consideration of losses," that is, proceeding without consideration of life, is a typically masculine expression. The only thing which matters is to put the bloodless ideologies into action. His main interests are not life and man but "progress," "science," "the fatherland" or some other abstraction. But the motherly woman places herself protectingly in front of life and shelters man in her love. Rouault labeled one of his most beautiful lithographs of the *"Miserere," "Bella matribus detestata,"* "mothers hate wars." Like the mother represented in it, holding her child in her arms, all mothers of the world want to protect life from the cold edge of the masculine sword. Mothers don't want to separate and rule, but to unite and heal.

All Misery Cries: "Mother!"

It will never be possible to eliminate suffering from the world. Man will always bruise himself against the limits set for him. There will always be sickness, misery and death. Sin, too, which causes physical and spiritual pain, will always be in the world. For the same reason, mankind will never cease to call the motherly woman who, because of her nearness, her presence, her patience and her ability of com-passion, is the natural helper. We are accustomed to say that our time is lacking in the serving professions, and with this we mean the acute shortage of personnel in social and hospital service. But what we lack more than everything else are motherly women, who, paid or unpaid, are willing to give more than just their hands to the service of the sick, weak and fallen; who give also their motherly hearts.

Meaning of the Mother-Tongue

According to his nature, the child, above all, needs motherliness. The smile in a child's face is a reflection. Children for whom the mother never had time, who were given only the "materially" necessary, are often for the rest of their life unable to radiate in their face this reflection of happiness. In the dialogue between mother and child the intellectual life is then roused, the miracle of language is happening. Thus we speak about a mother tongue, the language in which the mother first addressed the child and in which the child, if the mother taught him so, will pray for the rest of his life. Children whose mother did not have time for this loving address become intellectually and spiritually stunted. For, as we know, this motherly dealing with the child does not strive for a rational (grammatical or syntactical) perfection but opens up mysterious depths in which the intellect can never touch bottom.

Love for the Small

It is in this very way that the motherly woman bends towards everything small. She considers the small as valuable enough to give it her loving attention. She cares for it, covers and protects it from an icy grip. She opposes the centrifugal masculine powers, which are directed towards the outside and towards external ruling, with her love for inwardness; she opposes motion- and activity-hysteria with her joy in peacefulness, even in the seemingly insignificant.

Motherly Forgiving

Just as a mother does not tell the father in the evening every little mistake of the children, a true woman holds in life the office of mercifully covering. Man's drive goes towards information and discovery. Within him often lives a little prosecuting attorney who has to find out and accuse. No matter what the cost, the tiny splinter in the fellowman's eye must be found, photographed and publicized in headlines. But the motherly woman is inclined to overlook, to tolerate and to endure; she tends more to cover and enfold in the mantle of understanding and forgiving love. She knows that this love is often stronger than the evil, and that not the pilloring of sin but its merciful covering is what is full of meaning. For it is not so much the scandal-pregnant headlines which make the world better but rather sympathy and compassion; for a love which covers nakedness increases directly the power of the good.

Delivery Into Freedom

From all this it becomes clear that the most difficult task of the motherly woman is her obligation to deliver the child into freedom. By this I do not refer to the physical delivery of a child but to the spiritual delivery and releasing into freedom, which must take place a thousand times, a life long.

According to her very nature, the mother herself wants to keep. But the child's life demands that it soon grow into the realm of the father and then further into the realm of family, school, friendship and finally into his own marriage, and with this more and more away from the mother. Solomon recognized in his wisdom the true mother by her willingness to heroically renounce her right for the child's sake. Men fear the others' freedom; therefore they try to control and to limit it according to their own standards. But truly motherly women know also about the need to step aside, and to do so, if necessary, even in situations where children go ways feared wrong and leading to bitter experiences. Mothers know that even then a "free latitude" must be cultivated. This delivering ever anew is one of the most painful, yet one of the great mysteries of motherliness; for it is here that it finds its true fullness. Nothing indeed can hinder the child's maturity so much as a mother who in the guise of self-sacrifice which is actually egocentric protectiveness, does not deliver the child into freedom. On the other hand, there is no doubt that motherliness finds here, above all, its most spirit-ual form, the form most in accord with the Holy Spirit, since here the life-giving, preserving, protecting, healing and loving power finds its most free and fertile expression.

MOTHERLINESS AND MOTHERHOOD

Motherliness and Motherhood Are Not Identical

Motherliness as a spiritual and spiritualized attitude should not be confused with physical motherhood. True, physical motherhood can have an eliciting effect for motherly powers, which are dormant in every healthy girl, and which are usually intensively mobilized when the needs of one's own new-born stirs the awareness of the indigence of mankind in general. Physical motherhood frees and intensifies the basic motherly instincts.

Yet we shall state once more: motherhood and motherliness are not identical. Just as virginity does not consist in physical integrity, it likewise would be a mistake to think that mere physical motherhood or, even worse, the number of children, is a sure sign of motherliness. Thus when today we hear more and more the call for the motherly woman and, at the same time, the call for a limitation of physical motherhood, this is not necessarily a contradiction, where one cancels out the other, but is rather quite compatible, provided, of course, that we allow a difference of opinion as to its justification and expediency. Children may release motherliness within the mother, but it need not necessarily follow, as a mere glance at the newspaper confirms every day.

Praise of Motherhood

We have already spoken about the praise of fertility in the mythical images and symbols of the ancients. The Old Testament does not think differently. Woman becomes praiseworthy only through giving birth. The greatest happiness of the Jewish woman was physical motherhood. Her glory was to have many children, especially sons. Her spiritual powers of motherliness may have entered into her relationship with the children, but neither the family nor public life demanded it. But not to have borne children was a disgrace for a woman, and in most cases a sign of God's punishment. Accordingly, numerous offspring was the time and again quoted promise of God to the people. For children meant power, prestige and wealth. This aspect of the need of numerous offspring explains clearly the polygamy of the patriarchal times, and institutions, such as the levirate, a law, according to which a man whose brother died, leaving a widow without children, was obliged to marry her in order to provide offspring for the dead (Gen 38:8). Therefore the first son of this marriage carried the name of the dead and continued his line. Concretely this means: the men make use of the woman's fertility without taking into consideration her love or spiritual forms of motherliness. When in the books of Chronicles kings or other important persons are occasionally called by their mother's name, this is not done in order to honor the mothers, but because they were necessarily and obviously interested in differentiating brothers and step-brothers of polygamous families.

Towards the end of the Old Testament this concept seems to have somewhat broadened. True, in the book of Wisdom (e.g. 3:10-19) the motherly woman is not yet actually praised, but it is at least pointed out there that children can also turn out to be evil, in other words that the value of fertility is not an absolute one. One is tempted to interpret these verses as "not the quantity but the quality of children" — but even at the beginning of the New Testament, physical fertility is for Elizabeth, who grew old without children, the fulfillment of her life, for which she no longer dared to hope. Up to our day, Judaism holds the view that, because of the coordination of the sexes through creation, marriage is an obligation and woman must be fertile. For only thus the chosen people of the Covenant can continue existing. This naturalistic concept led among the early Jews to the ever impending apostasy into pagan Nature religions; and even the later on developed idea of God's marriage with the Jewish people could only mitigate but never completely abolish this concept.

Spiritual Fertility

It is only Christendom which sees the sexual from the viewpoint of a divine giving. The becoming-one-body points far beyond the biological sphere. If it takes place "in the

Lord" (Cor 3:18; Eph 5:22), the Lord, through this natural union, establishes a relationship between man and woman in which they can find God, serve the work of salvation and see fellow man in the right light. Nowhere in the New Testament is natural fertility of marriage demanded or made the yardstick of marital excellence. What matters to the Lord, is spiritual fertility. Matt 19:12 speaks about celibacy which is lived "by nature," "because of men," or "for the sake of the kingdom of heaven." Especially in this last form, spiritual fertility and spiritual motherliness are not only not excluded but rather intensified. One renounces marriage and physical fertility in order to serve the kingdom of God undividedly and thus with greater fertility.

Patriarchal and Pietistic Idealization

True, Paul goes back to the Old Testamental concept when he advises the younger widows to remarry, in order to "bear children," "rule their households," and "give the adversary no occasion for abusing us." But these admonitions are entirely based on the spirit of his time and are of a practical rather than an axiomatic character. More problematic seems to be his statement in 1 Tim 2:15. There he says: "Yet women will be saved by childbearing." Luther, whose image of God, and consequently also of man, was strongly influenced by Old Testament thinking, was very pleased with this idea, since he advocated a very patriarchal family structure and thus considered physical motherhood as the essential form of womanhood. Pietism followed his lead and gloried in the "many children of a mother," J. S. Bach's well-known "idyll" of a family with twenty children around the table. As we can see, Christendom did not strictly adhere to the pure and spiritual idea. We have only to look at Duerer's relentlessly realistic sketch of his mother's face in which we see the face of woman in

general, devastated by numerous childbirths and mis-
carriages, looking at us with burned out, wretched eyes.
Duerer wrote under the picture of this exhausted and totally
overburdened woman the striking words: "This, my godly
mother, bore and reared eighteen children, suffered great
poverty, horror and misery." One should not always look
only at genre-pictures of families with many children,
should not only promenade in unrealistic enthusiasm, but
should also look more often at this picture of a mother.
Was this woman fulfilled in marital companionship? Was
she at all able to activate the spiritual powers of motherliness dormant in her?

Someone might say that, after all, means of limiting or
of regulating the number of births were unknown at that
time. But the Egyptians, East Asiatics and Persians knew
such means three or four thousand years ago. We are, of
course, far from conveying or recommending, in restro-
spect, as it were, such knowledge to medieval women and
their descendants. Yet we would like to point out that it is
not so much backwardness or ignorance on the one hand
and familiarity with the knowledge of this or that possibility
of contraception on the other, which is decisive in this
question, but whether we uphold woman's dignity and freedom and her valuation as man's companion, or emphasize
her vocation of biological fertility.

The Woman Will Be Saved By Childbearing

With this we come back to the important exegetical
question whether in regard to an unlimited number of
children we can rightly refer to Paul's statement (1 Tim
2:15). The fact is, it has been quoted all too often in sermons and confessional exhortations. We read that even at
the beginning of our century for instance, the birthrate
jumped after great popular parish-missions. On the other
hand, the mere consideration that it is faith to which St.

Paul ascribes the decisive, salvific importance, should be enough to make us at least cautious in the exegesis of this question. A more thorough investigation should prove to us then that the above mentioned interpretation of "salvation through childbearing" is untenable. For we must start with the fact that Paul (2:13) speaks about Eve, that is, about woman in general. As a consequence of the sin in paradise, it became her hard destiny to painfully give birth to children. Yet, simultaneously attached to this curse is the promise that someday Eve's seed shall crush the head of the snake (Gen 3:15). Through her acceptance of the burden of childbearing, woman participates instrumentally in the realization of God's salvific will. Finally Mary, through the birth of the God-Man Jesus Christ, brings salvation to the world. Thus woman, if she willingly accepts her womanhood, cooperates, through faith, with God's salvation. This means in short: what, in a natural sense, is the burden of womanhood, becomes, through faith, the actual cause of her dignity within the divine plan of salvation. Understood in this way, woman, through childbearing, becomes more alive; while a wrong interpretation of our text leads to the notion that her childbearing leads to death. An idealistic overlay blocked the objective interpretation of Paul's concept, although in the context it is not difficult to find. When National Socialism with its apocryphal mysticism of blood and earth gave a decoration for having children; when communism bestows the title "mother hero," their reasons, of course, are not at all the praise of fruitful motherhood in Christian circles. Yet all have in common an idealizing superstructure which covers up the actual problem.

Tabooed Problem?

Are we here approaching a tabooed problem? We hope not; for, as has been truly said, after Christ's arrival, there should no longer be taboos in the world. Neither is there until the Lord's return a *causa finita*, that is, a problem which is absolutely solved. That a man or a group who breaks a felt or an established taboo, be ostracized from soicety, may be the case in the world, but within the Church this should certainly not be possible.

In Christendom, moral concepts, in particular, were in the course of centuries often exposed to spiritual tendencies which, even though originating in sources completely different from the New Testament, through their actual or apparent rigorousness passed themselves off as "more pious" and "more Christian." Hence, time and again, the theologian was and is obliged to separate and eliminate with one hand, and with the other to rediscover what is specifically Christian. This has never been done without a fight. Therefore today, when — rightly or wrongly — many a threshold of modesty is being transgressed, the theologian should face this our problem all the more earnestly, since it is still far from being solved; and farthest from the solution is the simple statement that a great number of children is necessarily a sign of piety and Christian thinking. The theologian should not take only a negative approach in proving that the nature of Christian morals does not consist in taboos antagonistic to love, but should, in a positive way, explain that these morals love love — more exactly, love in all its forms of expression; and that this love breathes the spirit of that freedom which is so much sought. For everything depends on whether the woman will find the possibility of a spirit-ual orientation in regard to motherhood and her responsible attitude towards it.

RESPONSIBLE MOTHERHOOD

Fundamentals

First: We have already emphasized that motherhood and

motherliness are not identical. The childless and the unmarried woman are also called to motherliness.

Secondly: We disavow the onesided, individualistically
and positivistically based arguments about the woman's
right to her body.

Thirdly: We reject a false, calculating attitude. It is just
as much an unnatural interpretation of the mystery of love
and life — a mystery which can be grasped only in its
wholeness — as are all the aforementioned idealistic fic-
tions.

Fourth: We reject a purely subjectively experienced love
which some mothers still recommend when they advise their
young married daughters: "make something out of your
life," "don't be foolish." Every "love" of this kind destroys
the marital *And*.

Fifth: We try to keep our distance from the widespread
fear of life which wants neither risk nor gain, and which
is attached to the present because of its helpless fear of
the future.

Finally — and this should be remembered as the most
important point — we emphasize that the loving union of
man and woman not only creates necessarily the will to
remain united for ever, since leading one another towards
maturity is the task of a lifetime, but that also the will to
parenthood is woven into the sexual union. As it is, the
inner readiness for the child is an essential part of the union
of the sexes. Every egotistic limitation, every degradation of
this union to the level of mere partnership leads to disturbances with grave consequences; the existence of which
prove the unnatural character of such behavior. Therefore
the Catholic Church rightly holds the view that in cases
where, in their agreement to marry, children are in principle
rejected and not desired, there is no marriage at all. This is
of its nature. Moreover, the child gives marriage a special

solidity and deepens the relationship of husband and wife in a way which those who without their fault have no children can compensate only by other fatherly or motherly activity.

Starting out from these principles we should approach the question of responsible motherhood which in today's much-cited "marriage difficulty" presents itself as an ever growing problem.

Religiously Disguised Submissiveness to Nature

There is a religiously masked submissiveness to nature which either leaves everything up to "God's way," or lets it go as it comes. We reject this glorified form of fatalism. As to the question of the meaning of work we often and rightly emphasize that man's kingly dignity consists in responsibly developing nature towards goals. This being so, it is hardly conceivable why then in this particular question of sex and reproduction man should accept only the course of nature. True, we reject a development of woman's personality which would close itself off from the man; but we believe that its healthy unfolding — a positive result of our time — does not permit that she must have children whenever the man's urge or "the course of nature" so desire. (Besides, the man himself today demands much more of woman in regard to companionship than was the case in former times.)

Voices of Modern Churchmen

Fifty, even thirty years ago, who in the Church would have said with Cardinal Gerlier: "Holy Scripture does not measure the perfection of a family according to the number of children"? Who, at that time, would have expected to hear high Church dignitaries maintain, as did the French Cardinal Archbishop on March 18, 1961, that the Catholic

Church does not rejoice in children regardless of the price? The same pastoral letter appeals to "reason, duty and conscience, to true love, to generosity in view of the gift of life, and to the obligation of deciding before God how many children they are able to bring up."[21] What bishop would have dared, at that time, to write, as Cardinal Koenig did in *"Presse"* on May 8, 1955, that, under certain circumstances, it could be a dictate of conscience to keep the number of children as small as possible, particularly in cases where it would be irresponsible to procreate more children then could be raised. True, this does not yet solve the problem. But the fact that one puts his finger on a raw spot is an indication that a question which seemed to be a *causa finita* wants to be heard.

The "Marriage Difficulty"

Inquiries made throughout the world as to questions which ought to be taken up by the Vatican Council, also proved the urgency of this problem.[22] Not only did desperate laymen ask for a more thorough study of this problem and for a better foundation of the hitherto existing positions, but theologians, too, made an approach in the same direction. Their motive was not criticism. Most of those who brought up the subject are above any suspicion. Their wishes and requests are not the result of irresponsible agreeing with the world, or of theological ignorance, but are the expression of a theological need and pastoral concern.

Can rigid conformists have any idea of the anguish of the confessional? Can they ever get honest information from the practice of confession in regard to this question — information which only in very rare cases one confrère passes to another *"sub sigillo"*? Can it ever be estimated how many people deprive themselves of eucharistic union with God because of false instruction, false education and false guidance? Let us think, too, of those millions who desire to love God more intimately but who, because of the strange ideas instilled in them, even to this day consider their marital love sinful and its forms of expression reprehensible. Because of this conflict, they reduce their relationship with God to a well-tempered lukewarmness.

The question as to what methods may be allowed for controlling the powers of nature in responsible motherhood is at the center of all care of souls. Superficialities can be regulated in one way or another, but love is the very heart of Christian being. Wherever love is forced to cool down, wherever there is a distinction between "true" and "false" expression of love, there is danger ahead — the danger that principles which are not in accord with the nature of love strangle the integral expression of love. Millions grow cold in the testimony of their love or go their own way in the belief that they have come to a gentleman's agreement with God or with the devil.

A Survey

Some time ago, a West-German theological magazine published a survey made by the Federal Republic[23] which strikingly shows the serious gap between the "teaching of the Church" and Catholic practice. 59 percent of the Catholics spoke clearly in favor of so-called contraception, 23 percent clearly against it. 18 percent of those questioned were without opinion. Among the regular Church-goers, 49 percent were against contraception; 21 percent without opinion. (Among church-going Lutherans, the shift in favor of contraception is considerable.) Thus it follows that of Catholics regularly attending Sunday Mass not even one out of three supported the teachings of the Church; and of those who participate irregularly not even one out of five. Besides this, we must keep in mind that also among the group of practicing Catholics there is often a wide gap between theory and practice. Confessors from far and wide could sing a song about this. Many of them long ago abandoned the method of desperate efforts and just keep silent, especially since, in the vast majority of the cases a lengthy and embarrassing questioning is needed to find out whether the "penitents" believe that what they routinely confess is actually sinful. We certainly do not want to slip into Kinsey's mistake and capitulate to statistics or even make them a norm. One of the differences between our survey and Kinsey's is without doubt the fact that our investigations were directed to a group with the same ideology. All those questioned knew the teachings of the Church. The second group sits beneath the pulpit Sunday after Sunday and doubtlessly also reads Catholic literature. Thus we can hardly deny that they want to love God. Nevertheless we find this discrepancy, as a result of which the birth rate in Germany is more or less equally "high" in Catholic and in non-Catholic marriages. The least one can conclude is that this group finds the arguments not sufficiently founded; an opinion shared by the Walberberg Dominicans (see 22), who are asking for a better foundation of sexual morals, and who certainly are not suspect of surrendering to a statistical morality.

The Problem of Abstinence

Theology accepts, at least in principle, a responsible control over the number of children. It offers as means either absolute abstinence from sexual intercourse in marriage or its restriction to woman's infertile days. Let us first consider absolute abstinence. This practice can easily lead to a number of difficulties which interfere considerably with the relationship of husband and wife; for, as we know, the sexual union of man and woman does not consist in the punctually determinable event but in a succession of looks and touches, of a harmony of many tender express-ions of love, the final culmination and most valid expression of which is the sexual union. Thus the close living-together of two people deeply in love with one another will either cause the desire of love's physical expression and the natural God-willed sexual excitement again and again to abate without fulfillment, and even at times to be brutally strangled — which leads to psychological disturbances — or else, that husband and wife deliberately live their love in a state of cool reserve and are forced to let their marriage grow poor and stunted. Their companionship turns into a living side by side instead of towards one another. Each dis-tracts himself from the other instead of turning to the other. Whoever has had the opportunity to observe such marriages knows that the denial was "heroic" only at the beginning. Later on both often adjust to the stunted state of their marriage. Their unfulfilled marital companionship mani-fests itself then only in nagging, escape, in work or in ill-nesses, or in envy of other happily married people.

The Calculating Momentum

The watching for the woman's periodic sterility brings a calculating momentum into marriage which should not be overlooked. In accordance with the whole tenor of the high song of love, one is tempted to rightly add to the qualities of love cited there: "Love does not calculate." Whoever intends a thorough study and an exact applica-tion of the rhythm methods which today the checking of body temperature makes more exact, doubtlessly needs a certain amount of time and intelligence to carry out this calculation. Now when even a great part of our European population cannot be expected to do this, how much less is it possible for the great multitude of uneducated people in the so-called underdeveloped countries who are also supposed to live morally. Besides, this method requires, for reasons of safety, that the sexual union — the spontaneous expression of oneness in love — be postponed or scheduled with a sliderule, as if love could be commanded. And, at the same time, one expects of the spouses the spiritual *salto mortale* of, in principle, desiring the child, while, "armed" with calendar and thermometer trying to exclude the possibility of conception.

Therapy for the Damages of Civilization

Much discussed of late is the proposition of the Jesuit, Stanislas de Lestapis,[24] which rests on the observation that the women of uncivilized nations cannot conceive another child during the first months after giving birth. He says that, because of civilizational influences, this biological expediency has been lost by our women; that nothing speaks against a therapeutic treatment of this loss and a reestablishment of the healthy natural condition through the dispensing of proper medicine. Boeckle, a moral theologian of Bonn, seems to share this opinion and to consider such medication justified during the first nine months after a delivery. On the other hand these drugs, already bombastically boomed by the advertising industry, are not yet sufficiently tested for side-and after-effects, and that is why sincere physicians and moral theologians feel obliged to advise utmost care. In this context, it is significant that already in Old Testament times weaning played an important role. Abraham gave a great feast on the day of Isaac's weaning (Gen 21:8). Exegetes suppose that he was about two or three years old. Likewise the Maccabean mother says to her son that she had nourished him at her breast for three years (2 Mach 7:27). At the same time, however, these examples present a new difficulty. What gives us the right to establish an average period of nine months during which it should be permitted to take correcting pills? Are there not enough primitive races whose women nurse their children for several years? If we refer to Gen 38:9 to forbid onanistic sexual intercourse (although, as we know, Onan was submitted to such severe punishment only because he broke the law of the levirate marriage) should not the quotation in 2 Mach 7:27 be taken just as seriously, and contraceptives be allowed for a period of three years? But a moral theology which wants everything to be minutely established, and which fears nothing more than the breakthrough of principles which are expansible, will probably, as a consequence, also reject these devices; besides, these devices do not solve the acute problem but could at best mitigate it.

Temporary Sterilization

Recently, in connection with the rapes which occurred in the Congo, the question arose whether temporary sterilization would be permissible. It seems that official and semi-official attitudes are changing somewhat in this regard. And why not? As we know, there was even a time when a papal bull (*Summis desiderantes*) stated that there are relationships of devils with human beings; a statement which later on, however, was clearly and expressly revoked. Several councils declared the charging of interest a damnable sin: today, the Church also charges interest. Other questions, as, for instance, the correctness or incorrectness of the *comma Johanneum*, needed scarcely 50 years to be tacitly allowed to be discussed. Why then should not opinions regarding the problem of controlled temporary sterilization also change? As recently as February 22 1940, the *Sanctum Officium* answered the question of the permissibility of sterilization with an unambiguous *"negative."* On September 12, 1958, Pius XII defined it more precisely, explaining that sterilizing means be permitted if the primary purpose of their use is therapeutic and sterilization consequently merely a secondary aim. Today, three leading Roman moral theologians (P. Pallazini, secretary of the Congregation of the Council, F. Hurth, S.J., and F. Lambruschini) declare in an expert opinion that it could not be absolutely sinful to use drugs with the intention of preventing the consequences of an imminent rape; that a temporary sterilization is forbidden only if causally connected with the will to marital intercourse. To my mind, this argument is not valid. If it is true what gynecologists long since confirm, that often there are more rapes within marriage than outside of it,[25] how could one justify the refusal of sterilization methods to tormented and frequently raped women?

We Mark Time

What we have said so far leads to two observations: The so-called marriage difficulty is a universal one. It is not one which is only written on paper but it burns itself daily anew into those affected: into married people and their pastors alike. Secondly, the solutions offered are only partly realizable, only with reservations and not by everyone. In the Christian Family groups for instance not only nothing new can be said in this direction but in most cases no actual solution can be shown at all. We are marking time. For me at least it has been always a painful experience when such groups meet together with high expectations, only to separate again afterwards, more or less disappointed. Whatever was said was already known before. Married people know the Church's viewpoint. They distinguish only between the Church's individual representatives the priests, who show more or less understanding for their difficulty, who "treat" their worries with more or less tact and aptitude, and who apply various pastoral methods and norms.

Is A Good Intention Decisive?

One group of priests proceeds from the assumption that it is wrong to judge an act merely "as such." That rather the intention should play the main role in its evaluation; for, according to early Christian conviction, only the intention makes an act good or evil. In this context great men are cited like Chrysostom, Augustine, Bernard of Clairvaux and Thomas Aquinas. It is true, they continue, that evil means do not become good by a good intention; but, on the other hand, to use contraceptives does not at all imply in every case the bad intention of deliberately refusing the blessing which God has joined to marital union. They are rather used with the quite justifiable intention to give life only to the number of children which is in accordance with the woman's physical condition and the family's social situation. Accordingly one could in this case speak of a material but not of a formal sin; especially where the conscience of the spouses is in "invincible error."

To Let It Happen?

Other priests take the viewpoint which, concisely described, means to let happen, for pastoral reasons, what is ultimately inevitable. They refer to an address given by Pius XII on October 29, 1951, in which the Pope said: "In cases where serious reasons demand a heroic abstinence from any full exercise of the natural capacity, external expressions of the most intimate tenderness are allowed even at the risk that what is ordinarily sinful may happen unintentionally." Thus here, too, the emphasis is given to the intention, and the marital integral tenderness and love is underlined. Modern moral theologians as, for instance, Leclercq and Fleckenstein, share this opinion. (By the way, when the Theatine, Antonio Diana, at the beginning of the 17th century, held the same view, St. Alphonsus Liguori, the Church's official moral theologian, accused him of laxity.) Of course, none of these theologians would consider it justifiable for the priests and confessors to give advice in this direction. Thus the recipe is to say nothing and to let things happen, and to keep the question of subjective guilt open.

Mercy Before Justice

A third form of pastoral treatment is to speak not so much about the ordinance of the law but rather about God's mercy. By this is meant that God will certainly be a "merciful judge" for him who had prayerfully examined his conscience and who often sees no other solution but one which, according to the ordinance of the law, is sinful. They hold that in this case God will "temper justice with mercy": that the law is the power of the sin, but that its obligating character is either cancelled by the core of the gospel, or in principle put under the aspect of forgiveness. This viewpoint, which is held primarily in Lutheran circles (Bonhoeffer), makes high demands on the formation and strength of conscience. Other theologians do not go so far and see in God's tempering-justice-with-mercy a kind of emergency regulation, in effect until science is able to provide a proper solution of the problem.

Unsatisfying "Solutions"

All those solutions and pastoral methods which we have mentioned are actually unsatisfactory. Sincere theologians know this all too well; the "affected" marriages experience this every day anew. For none of these solutions is complete. Besides it is scarcely flattering for married people to know that they commit only a material or objective sin and that God "tempers justice with mercy." With this interpretation their marital love continues being a blemish, unbearable for one who honestly and sincerely loves God. Does this have to be so? To conclude let us draw up, out of our earlier considerations, a few principal viewpoints which perhaps may give a lead, although they do not pretend to actually solve this pressing problem once and for all.

Life-Formation in Love Instead of Casuistry

After so many well-meant attempts it seems justifiable to ask whether a solution can be found at all within the hitherto used channels. Nobody can maintain for instance, that in our modern, highly differentiated, social and economic structure with its rapid change, final solutions are available for all the questions concerning the seventh commandment. Certainly everybody knows that he should not steal or defraud, that he must be just and, as a Christian, love poverty. But this says nothing concretely, for instance, in regard to the permission to buy stocks, in regard to agrarian reform, to a just wage and the content of the "social package"; Holy Scripture cannot give us immediate information. These questions must be solved through an enlightened theology, within a positive and objective ethical Christian framework. Yet we find at times rather conflicting ideas of the alleged questions — also among Christians who read scripture and consult their consciences. Who wants to beat here constantly with the sin-club? How could such an attitude be justified? Should not what is right in social and economic questions be also fair in questions of marital life-formation? When, for instance, a two-volume set of moral theology treats the sixth commandment (*"Punctum puncti"*) in a separate volume twice as volumin-

ous as the others, the author's motives could be justifiably
questioned. Such texts may be a help and a support for
confession-hearing baroque priests, but they are of little
use for a positive life-formation of the faithful. Are we
surprised then when Christians, who seem to have successfully maneuvered the slalom race through the set up
markers, believe that they have reached the "maturity of
Christ"? Can we be surprised when such people after years
of laxity and indifference towards God and their fellowman, come to the confessional and cannot remember a sin?
Is it not necessary "to leave behind the innumerable, mostly negative moral directives in the style of Old Testament
legal justice which are often alien to medical and psychological knowledge" (O. Rigler),[22] and to contribute more
to a positive formation of marital life in love? Molina
and the Jesuits of his time recognized very clearly that
it is not difficult to establish generally formulated and
merely negative axioms. But it is more difficult to breathe
positive life into those formal principles untouched by life,
and this means in our case to call for the formation of a
fulfilled life and to permit creative initiative to unfold itself in love. Whoever constantly and anxiously suspects
these creative powers of love cannot be surprised when, in
the long run, they languish and grow cold.

Consideration Under the Aspect of Wholeness

It seems imperative to me to acquire a biblical attitude
towards this pressing problem and to see the entire sexual
life as an undivided whole rather than individually and
separately to evaluate the many different acts comprised by
this whole. A more or less correct ethical valuation of the
individual acts is possible only in the context of the total
idea of marriage of both partners. For "the eye of the law"
completely fails to see that the individual act receives its

positive or negative value only through the basic attitude of the spouses towards God's blessing connected with their sexuality. If there is no will to parenthood; if, for reasons of pleasure or comfort, they despise God's blessing, their entire sexual life is sinful, and herewith also every individual act. If they accept God's blessing or even have already expressed this acceptance by a number of children corresponding to their physical and social conditions, no one is authorized to judge but God, with whom they are united in prayer and in examination of conscience. In this sense it may be necessary to speak, instead of many individual sins, rather of *the* sin which is a basic condition of man. By such, through his own free will, he deliberately turns away from God and towards the world. In most cases it is this basic attitude which St. Paul refers to when speaking of sin in the singular. St. John seems to know only children of the light and children of the darkness. These theologians are far from applying a meticulous evaluation of the individual act. Grace, which is also spoken of in the singular, is opposed to and cancels out sin; through grace, life is conveyed. This explains John's statement that he who abides in love abides, in principle, in life. For grace and love are identical. It seems to us the special task and vocation of the spiritual woman to live, responding to divine grace, this attitude of wholeness in the harmony of love and life, and to teach the rationally analysing man.

Development in Freedom and Love

"*Ubi caritas et amor, Deus ibi est.*" Wherever this one and that one love, there is God. Considering these words, who would assume the right to give importance to punctilious means and forms of expression of a love which deserves this name only when it totally seeks the other in whom — according to his own word — Christ manifests himself, in order, unselfishly, to fuse with him into the holy oneness which is the goal of all loving desire? Who would assume the right to hinder the unfolding of the creative powers of this love and to establish laws which demand a constant scrutinizing, a constant squinting, and which, as is proved, leads to coldness and to the death of this love? Is it not true that love, above all, needs freedom? It is not by chance that the Holy Spirit is at once the spirit of love and of freedom. Are we Christians forced to become mere consumers of leftovers of freedom instead of being producers of freedom and its creative fashioners? *"La loi de Dieu ne s'addresse pas a des automates"* (de Lestapis). "The law of God does not address the automaton," that is, puppets, whose "acting" is worthless, performed on strings. Man is the king of this creation for the sole reason that he forms his life meaningfully with his intellect and free will and within the framework of the great order, and not according to laws which "intervened that the offense might abound" (Rom 5:20). Even the solutions pointed out by the casuists involve love and a free responsible decision in order to render them morally valuable. The only difference is that a purely casuistic interest is not oriented towards a positive formation of this love but rather towards its fences.

However, the building and guarding of fences is again a typically masculine interest. It was not without good reason that in the excessively masculine age of the Old Testament the narrow-meshed law "ripened" into a terrible perfectness; not without good reason do the laws in all male societies play the top role and go hand in hand with a suspicion of naturally creative powers. But without a free unfolding of these creative powers, and above all of the powers of love, a true marital life is almost impossible. Because of her spiritual nature, it is above all the woman to whom these powers are given, to whom they are coordinated. Just as the Holy Spirit refuses to let canals be dug through which he may come, since he "blows where he wills" (John 3:8); woman, too, breathes the spirit of free creative love in the marital relationship. The man may see to it that love does not grow rampant; but it is woman's irreplaceable task to keep love from being smothered and frozen, from becoming stale and uncreative in the Procrustean bed of the laws. Masculine concerns have been taken seriously long enough. The time has come to take seriously also the woman's concerns. Then I think, we would become happier, more human, and, at the same time, more closely united with God.

MARY, THE MOTHERLY WOMAN

We had planned to let the Church show us a valid model for each of the three forms of feminine life. While we are still waiting for a saintly companion, there is no more radiant example and model either for the virgin or for the mother than Mary. Just as she was totally virgin she also was totally mother.

The Mother of God

The Council of Ephesus expressly gave Mary the title "Mother of God." Her whole life, her entire love, belonged to the child. More so than others, the affectionate German temperament has expressed Mary's motherly happiness in ever new paintings: She holds the child in her arms, nourishes him at her breast and gives him her tender smile. The Holy Spirit did not come to her as a representative of the heavenly Father, but he overshadowed her in order to effect in her the state, the condition, of being-the-mother. Her entire life was a service of the life she was chosen to give. Every day she was the "servant of the Lord" (Luke 1:38).

The Mother of Sorrows

But Mary not only gives life to the Son, she gives, like all true mothers, the Son to the world. In Christian iconography, we find the theme of the mother holding the Son in front of her and giving him to the world and to mankind even before we find the representation of her happy motherhood. In these pictures mother and child do not face one another but both look in the direction of mankind standing before them. Hence it is not a dialogue between Mary and Jesus but between Jesus and the devout viewer, between the Lord and his needy world. In fact, it seems that already in the first days after his birth, the mother began to feel the pain of the child's severing, of her motherly letting go. The sword of sorrow which many times pierced her heart stands between the mother and the child from the moment that she heard the words alluding to their separation: "Did you not know that I must be about my Father's business?" (Luke 2:49). Thus the mother of the seven sorrows and the seven swords gave her Son away time and again, until, in the most sorrowful hour of her life, she holds her dead Son in her lap. Guided by the Holy Spirit, not once did she block his way, not once did she even make the gesture of keeping him. As the mother of sorrows she is, at the same time, the mother of enduring and releasing love who like all mother who release, died a thousand deaths in releasing, and have stepped back into the mystery of the anonymity of all mothers, which is the mystery of the veil.

The Madonna with the Sheltering Mantle

It was above all German medieval art which represented the veil of the virgin, and this veil of the mother who steps aside, as a mantle under which afflicted mankind can see refuge. Just as a hen gathers its young under its protecting wings, Mary the mother gathers all anguish of the weak all misery of the afflicted. Her motherly protecting shelter is, as it were, an asylum which, according to an ancient law, was excluded from prosecution; it is the refuge-keep where the unprotected can take sanctuary. Man in misery, that is, man living in a foreign land, knows himself outlawed. The madonna with her protecting mantle gives him sheltering, motherly warmth. When, on Christmas 1942, in the hell of Stalingrad a German Lutheran minister drew with charcoal on the walls of his bunker this same lovely picture of Mary, for him a symbol of protection in the midst of death and unimaginable terror, he not only created an impressive monument to all motherly sheltering, but he also spontaneously found in Mary the most beautiful expression for it.

Like Mary, So The Church

"Like Mary, so the Church," says Ivo of Chartres. Together with him, many theologians point out that the Church represents herself in a Marian way. The *Ecclesia* of the cathedral in Strassburg is built in a virginal form lifting its chalice upward towards the cross to receive the redeeming blood of the Lord. The second council of Lyon calls the Church "our virginal Mother," since she passes on the graces she received and thus gives birth in her womb to the supernatural, true life. An inscription on the baptistry of the Lateran rightly says that the Church brings forth out of her womb sons whom she conceived through the breath of God. When in the Easter Vigil the power of the Holy Spirit is called down upon the baptismal water, that is, the motherly womb of the Church, this Holy Spirit effects in her the state of motherliness which wants to give, and only to give.

But as a true mother, the Church also wants to protect this life. A mother does not say to the children: "Here there are many bottles: concentrated vinegar and raspberry juice, sulphuric acid and milk. You are big enough. Go on and drink what you like!" A mother labels or even locks up the poison since she wants to avoid once and for all that the children will suffer damage. Likewise the motherly caring Church, when lovingly exercising her pastoral office, calls the poison poison, and the devil devil. The state, which in Germany, for the same reason, we rightly also call "father state," uses other, harder, masculine means. The Church has never wanted to consider herself hard in a masculine sense. Therefore the masculine name *"Thiasos,"* which means "religious festival association", proposed for the Church by Eusebius, did not come through. "Is it possible that breaking through here are human fear and the longing not to be at the mercy of the masculine "figure" of the State or imperium in all areas of life, especially not in the most sensitive and spiritually deepest one the religious area?"[26] Above all, in her protectiveness, the Church wants to be a mother.

Just as the pain of delivery and separation is part and parcel of all true motherhood, the Church, too, knows about this sword of sorrow. To leave the warmth of the motherly nest and to grow mature are identical. Fathers may force a unity, may give orders and punish. Mothers suffer and expiate, but they lovingly release into freedom.

BIBLIOGRAPHIC REFERENCES

1. W. Moll, *Father and Fatherhood*, Fides, 1966.
2. O. Schneider, *Die Macht der Frau.*
3. L. Ziegler, *Apollons letzte Epiphanie.*
4. *Apokryphen zum Neuen Testament* (Sammlung Dietrich).
5. Bulgakoff, *Kapitel ueber die Trinitaet.*
6. J. Tyciak, *Mariengeheimnisse.*
7. L. Ziegler, *Ueberlieferung.*
8. G. von Le Fort, *The Eternal Woman*, Bruce, 1962.
9. P. Evdokimov, *Die Frau und das Heil der Welt.*
10. M. J. Scheeben, *Handbuch der Dogmatik II.*
11. H. de Lubac, *The Splendor of the Church*, Paulist.
12. H. Bremond, *Das wesentliche Gebet.*
13. F. Hillig, *Vom Schauspiel der Messe, Stimmen der Zeit,* August 1947.
14. T. Haecker, *Schoenheit, ein Versuch.*
15. A. Nygren, *Agape and Eros*, Westminster.
16. Adam, *Der Primat der Liebe*, Kevelaer, 1940.
17. L. Bloy, *Briefe an seine Braut.*
18. G. Marcel, *homo viator.*
19. D. V. Hildebrand, *Ehe und Uebervoelkerung,* in *"Stimmen der Zeit."*
20. Herbert Marcuse, *Eros and Civilization*, Beacon, 1955.
21. Herder-Korrespondenz, 15. Jg, S. 351.
22. *Umfrage zum Konzil, "Wort und Wahrheit,"* Sonderheft Oktober 1961.
23. *Trierer Theologische Zeitschrift*, 70. Jg, Heft 6.
24. S. de Lestapis S.J., *Geburtenregelung-Geburtenkontrolle.*
25. H. Ellis, *Monatsschrift fuer Geburtshilfe*, 1889/9.
26. R. Graber, *Maria im Gottgeheimnis der Schoepfung, ein Beitrag zum metaphysischen Wesen des Christentums.*

Agrapha   words of Jesus which are not handed down in the canonical gospels

Androgynous   masculine and feminine sex resident in one and the same person

Anima   literally: soul; here: a term of depth psychology. Means the psychic disposition toward sexus and eros, which shows up in dream symbols

Antiphysis   counter-nature

Apocryphal   literally: hidden; also: unauthentic, for instance, unauthentic, non-canonical scripture

Arcanum   a secret

Ascesis   systematic exercise towards moral life; often: penitential exercise, abstinence

Athos   republic of monks on the eastern peninsula of Chalcidice; the "holy mountain", of high reputation among all the Orthodox

Autarchy   self-contentment, independence

Basilian liturgy   a form of eastern liturgy

Biologism   unjustified transference of biological concepts and knowledge into other sciences

Cabalism   a form of Jewish mysticism

Casuistry   a branch of moral theology which applies general principles to the individual case of conscience; originally designed as a help for confessors, it became later on accessible also to laymen and led through many excesses to scruples and psychological difficulties

Cathari   literally: those who are pure; much opposed, medieval sect hostile to the body

Comma Johanneum   the passage, 1 John 5:7, lacking in all Greek manuscripts and today generally considered as added later on

Debitum   duty, service

Deisis   icon frequently found in the Eastern Church which shows Christ between Mary and John the Baptist

Encratites   literally: those who live abstinent; an early Christian sect which demanded among other things abstention from marriage

Eschatology   doctrine of the final things

Ethnology   science of the races of mankind

Exegesis   explanation of Holy Scripture

Flammeum   red nuptial veil

Gaea   the earth-mother

Gnosis   literally: knowledge; within Christendom, a movement influenced by pagan philosophy, which rejects the doctrine that the Logos became man

Homo faber   the working man

Hypertrophy   overnourishment, exaggeration

Hypostasis   a concept of the doctrine of God and Christ; it means the last bearer of an individual nature equal to "person"

Iconostasis   wooden partition in Eastern churches, adorned with icons, which separates the nave from the bema

Iconography   description and explanation of pictures

Jahwe   name of God "I am who am"

Jansenism   religious movement in France of the seventeenth century: a concept exaggerating the original sin which led to an anthropological pessimism, doubt of salvation, excessively strict morality and, as a practical consequence, infrequent reception of the sacarments

Laxism   moral theological tendency which considers an action as morally allowed even though there is only little probability of its rectitude; condemned by the Church

Messalians   enthusiastic sect in Mesopotamia between the third and the 14th century

Metahistorical   beyond what is historically accessible

Mystery cult   pagan, mostly secret, cult, in which the mythical fate of a God is represented in words and acts (for instance, Cybele, Isis, Dionysis, Mithras)

Myth   an old tradition which, mostly in poetic and picturesque language, tells about primeval events (myths of the creation, of gods, and salvation bearers)

Neo-Platonism   last phase of the ancient philosophy of predominantly platonic character

Orante feminine symbolic figure in early Christian art, arms outstreched, palms up in a supplicating posture

Pansexualism theory and behavior according to which sexuality is the root of all psychic activity; the meaning of life is seen in an unrestricted activation of the sexual

Phallus the male organ (Greek)

Pietism movement of renewal within German Protestantism of the 17th and 18th century, which demands an interior movement by Christ, personal conversion and a strict moral regime

Pneuma spirit

Polarity tension between contrary yet correlated and complementary forces

Priapus in Asia Minor, demon of fertility

Prometheus Greek mythical figure who stole the fire which the gods withheld from man; since then the incarnation of rebellion

Psyche soul

Puritanism a movement within English Protestantism which wanted to give back to the Church the original purity in doctrine and life

Ratio reason

Rationalism ideology which tries to explain everything by reason

Rigorism a fixed, narrowminded spiritual attitude; unenlightened enthusiasm for an impersonal law

Secularization transference from ecclesiastical to civic use

Sanctum Officium congregation of cardinals for the preservation of the purity of doctrine in Catholic faith and morals

Sophia doctrine doctrine of God's wisdom held by pious Russian thinkers

Spiritualism actually: acceptance of the reality of the spirit; often: an attitude directed against bodiliness and sexuality

Subordinatianism a condemned doctrine subordinating the Son to the Father in the Trinity

Sub sigillo under the seal (of secrecy of confession)

Taboo a law mostly of religious origin, which prohibits certain things or persons to be spoken of, to be looked at or to be touched

Triad a union of three